CIVIC
REVOLUTION

A CITIZEN'S GUIDE

RIC CASALE

D1330754

Matador
9 Priory Business Park,
Wistow Road, Kibworth Beauchamp,
Leicestershire. LE8 0RX
Tel: 0116 279 2299
Email: books@troubador.co.uk
Web: www.troubador.co.uk/matador
Twitter: @matadorbooks

ISBN 978 1789018 608

British Library Cataloguing in Publication Data.
A catalogue record for this book is available from the British Library.

Printed and bound in the UK by TJ International, Padstow, Cornwall

Matador is an imprint of Troubador Publishing Ltd

To those who live in towns and cities.

Contents

Foreword

In the 4th century BC, Plato, the father of Western philosophy, had a profound insight which was that education should take place outdoors among woods and gardens to remind us constantly of the organisation and relationships of the natural world, and so be informed by observation and understanding of it. He chose as his first school site the garden of the Athenian hero, Academus, and it became known as the Academia and so heralded the dawning of what would become Academic thinking.

Two thousand years later, this intellectual insight would provide the background to the Age of Enlightenment, where intellectual life would become consumed by a curiosity with interrelationship and the ordering of all things, to better understand their nature and thereby see the world anew. First seen as something of wonder and revelation, the view of the world inexorably shifted into an approach that saw this new knowledge as being at the service of human utility: a world interpreted by the emergent economic philosophy of Capitalism as an opportunity to exploit nature in the name of growth.

Charles Darwin's *On the Origin of Species* comfortingly provided a framework that was hijacked to imply that survival of the fittest, through competition, was the Natural Order of things. This made a revolutionary insight palatable to a religious culture that otherwise would have seen such thoughts as a challenge to its foundations. The tragic irony is that Darwin's key observations revealed the extraordinary way in which life on earth succeeds by adapting to the myriad niches on offer. While it is true that extinctions follow the inability to find a niche to adapt to, he was describing a world of interrelationships with no waste, a system or systems that maintained a balance within the natural boundaries of what the planet could sustain.

Science, as a word, would not be coined until the 1830s. Up until then the study of natural phenomena and their interrelationships was called Natural Philosophy. Newton, Darwin, Lyell and Huxley would all have called themselves Natural Philosophers. The age of specialism cannibalised this overarching title and broke it down into the silos of "isms" and "ologies" we know today. Headlong reductionist pursuit of territory for study rendered the overarching understanding of natural systems old fashioned, and it is only over the last twenty or so years that we realise the wrong turn we have taken.

How ironic that Plato's original thinking could have been so catastrophically undermined by the very institutions that took his name – Academia. At the same time, how heartening it is to see the ferment in the tech world as they rediscover again what we have come to call "ecology". At the time of writing, the big tech companies are hiring ecologists for premiums above those of coders, realising that binary algorithms have their limits.

Recently, on climbing one of the biggest trees on earth, in Sequoia Crest in the Sierra Nevada Mountains of California, I had, in my terror, a moment of great clarity. As my sticky palms clung to the soft bark I turned to thinking of this Giant Sequoia's great age. It was approximately 4,500 years old. To the best of my limited knowledge this particular tree had outlived the flowering and demise of 37 civilisations, each populated by an Establishment that would probably have had a relatively similar number of intelligent people to our own, yet, in each case the Establishment catastrophically got it wrong.

The reason we should be hopeful today, is that for the first time ever, we have a line of sight to our global interconnectedness, and our young people see their interests as not defined by narrow boundaries. At the same time, science is revealing aspects of life on earth that were formerly thought to be suited, and relevant only, to specialists in their blinkered silos. As we are coming to understand such expansive things as the micro-biomes inside ourselves, and the interconnected fungal chains in the soil beneath our feet, we are living through the greatest revolution in understanding the nature of life itself.

This book is important and well timed. It feels as if we are standing at a boundary which will define us not simply by a new Anthropocene era. Many are talking of meaning and purpose, and while the word spiritual is probably not quite right, there is a hunger for something that gives us direction with confidence. The lodestone for this emerging culture is deep ecology. The book's urgent argument that the world needs a revolution in thinking is undoubtedly true. It is also true that no fact changes the world; only a story can do that. In this story, cities are the nexus and people are the agents of change, and the "ecological genius" of the city is understood to be both environmental and social – each dependent on the other and inextricably interwoven.

Civic Revolution is about the clash between our culture and wellbeing, and how this dissonance might be resolved. Ric answers a fundamental question for our time: how is it possible to mend the broken link between prosperity and a sustainable future? We should first ask whether in a well-balanced society the need to consume represents the only agency we feel we have, and is it possible that, with the return of a more holistic overview of life, a restating or revisioning of the values of community and deeper sense of belonging, those urges are tempered? A friend once memorably remarked when discussing education, "The question isn't what sort of planet are we leaving our children. We should ask instead, what sort of children should we be leaving the planet?" Plato would have agreed.

Sir Tim Smit
January 2019

Introduction

What is happening in national politics makes me angry and I am not alone. We live precariously in an unsustainable twenty-first century global economy and an unstable environment. And yet our true calling to lift these shadows is deadened by the collective fear of breaking a broken system. The antidote to this lack of courage and vision is to do what we can to change the immediate world around us. Our livelihood depends on many things, not least a different perspective and broader aspirations. The good news is that the systemic change we need is fractal by nature: it requires leadership at every level of society.

Government can be pushed by citizens to make revolutionary changes, often with the help and organisation of impassioned social activists. They advocate fundamental change resolutely on behalf of their fellow citizens, agitating from outside the system. We need these committed individuals and their energy: they wake us up, and if we don't wake up we become complicit.

Most of us are not activists, but all of us are citizens. This is a guide for us to take direct action locally, to spend our energy creating meaningful change where we live. Active citizenship is about finding new ways to make our city the seat of the solution and create non-linear change. It is about navigating the tension between our anger with this broken system and an appreciation of how it works. It is about implementing solutions to the problems that matter, no matter what happens.

Labelled as consumers and defined by our work, we forget our role as citizens. Our individual civic powers have atrophied to such an extent that we have become illiterate in civics. Civics boils down to the simple question of who decides. No one knows the city where you live better than you, so why let someone else take the decisions? I use the term "city" (here and throughout the book) loosely as shorthand for a place with a relatively high degree of urban-ness. Official city status does not matter: it's the density and proximity of people that count, not physical boundaries or population size.

A friend of mine joked that it takes a mid-life crisis to write a good book. Our mid-life crisis could not be any bigger. Does humanity have a future measured in as many generations as its past? I don't have the answer. However, this is not a sweeping book about the fall of human civilisation. It is more personal. Too many of us think we don't have the option of taking our lives in different directions. But the reality is that you do have this power at any point in time. You just have to use it.

Civic Revolution is about the power we have as citizens to reinvent the city or place where we live and in doing so create a more sustainable future for everyone. The links are broken between people and places, past and present, imagination and reality. By restoring these connections a new narrative for prosperity emerges, one of lasting social and economic vitality locally, for human civilisation as a whole.

The backdrop to the story is the predicament of humankind, a quest for endless economic expansion in a world of finite resources and planetary boundaries. It feels like we are living through the end of the world as we have overstepped our own red lines and triggered the tragedy of the mass extinction of species and the chaos of climate change. We tell ourselves that new technology will be the solution, when the story of our time is not one of technology disruption but of behaviour disruption.

Recognising the need for a new narrative, in the second part of the book I look beyond the role of nation states and rediscover that people's loyalty to their city has deeper roots. Cities are rising up once more, and the perspective I take is unapologetically urban. Over half of the world's population already lives in cities, and over two billion more people will be living in cities within the next thirty years. This momentum is earth-shattering. Nonetheless, the urbanisation of humanity – the single biggest cause of global warming and mass extinction – is potentially the principal solution. The ecological genius of the city enables us to live better while consuming less and polluting less. Yet it remains a vast, largely hidden power.

In the third part of the book I sift for clues in our past that shape the proposed change in direction. The focus of previous industrial revolutions was on labour productivity – producing more stuff with fewer employees – with scant regard for the inefficient use of natural resources or the social cost of unemployment. The civic revolution turns this world upside down, and inverts making people more productive into making natural resources and ecosystems more productive. Intellectual revolutions in the past have stirred our imagination and reshaped our social, rational and political behaviour. This one is no different, appealing to our civic state of mind and the hope of prosperity that can last.

In this citizen's guide, I identify a coherent set of beliefs that cut through the doubts about whether or not to take action, and what kind of action we can take. I set out the imperatives we face as a society and how our attitudes to civic life can make a world of difference. Instead of a political philosophy of the left or right, the beliefs are representative of a new stage. They are perhaps the universal design principles for how cities should be built to last, and how citizens should bring these places to life in order to discover richness.

Rural populations are entangled in the negative impacts of people migrating to cities and the positive effects of city influence on surrounding areas. These populations outside cities are a formidable force for environmental good, under pressure from the distal demands of urban centres. Nonetheless, civic revolution encompasses everyone: the civic attitudes needed are the same everywhere, although the actions we take are specific to the place where we live. In this story I focus on the civic actions of city dwellers, a story pushed to the margins by national politics, macroeconomic growth and technology innovation. There is another story to be told about the leadership role that rural communities can play, and their kinship with urban populations.

I draw lessons from the civic initiatives of individuals and the leadership shown by individual cities; from examples of good urban governance and design; and from our shared history and its trajectory. However, I do not dwell on the social science of collective change or the technological challenges and opportunities that could catalyse this change, as this book is not aimed at the academic, scientific or engineering communities. Instead, you are the protagonist. You are either the hero or the villain, but not a bystander.

We have already exceeded the planetary boundary for greenhouse gas emissions, at our peril. In the fourth part of the book I explore how we can reinvent the economy using our power and return to relative safety. A restorative economy consists of clean growth and circular economies. I consider these aims as two sides of the same coin: our source of energy will not be stable unless we reduce our dependence on extractive industries; the economy will not be stable unless we reduce our dependence on extracting primary materials. Citizens play a vital role in this transition. Empowered by control over our energy supplies, we become producers as well as consumers of renewable energy. If we are resourceful in outlook and actions, then we can address the fundamental issue of overshoot, the cause of our ecological crisis.

By killing too many species too quickly, we have also exceeded a second core planetary boundary. Biodiversity provides the basis for our survival, producing all our food, cleaning the air and water around us, keeping our climate in balance. In the fifth part of the book I look at saving life, recognising the dire consequences of mass extinction on biodiversity and on our livelihood. We cannot live in cities independently of biodiversity; our dependency on biodiversity enables us to live in cities.

I explore ingenious new ways in which citizens are integrating nature into their city lives, and how we are embedding ecosystems into our urban spaces. I look at how people are taking the initiative to be more conservative in their use of energy, water and land, reducing their city's footprint and its impact on biodiversity. We see how communities can organise themselves to manage and protect common natural resources successfully, for the common good. Without doubt, it is a big shift in our perspective to accommodate very real natural boundaries instead of attempting to extend them to meet more of our demands.

We need a narrative that is not just an escape route from danger. Change that lasts comes from hope, not fear. The aim of discovering richness in the sixth part of the book is to fulfil our aspiration for a prosperous future. Cities are the best places not simply for the economic elite to roost but for a lasting kind of prosperity that benefits many people. Public affluence represents this alternative route to a rich quality of life, and is a manifestation of the humanity we can bring to bear in our cities. We see how there is no sustainability without diverse and inclusive places in cities where we share our finite resources more humanely, while nourishing the human spirit.

I gather all these threads together in the closing chapter, with the aim of inspiring revolution and putting ourselves back into the narrative. Nation states will continue their bids for wider influence and regional hegemony; corporations will tighten their grip on the public domain; individuals will claim power in their various roles from presidents to chief executives to celebrities. We cannot wait for any of them to lead the charge towards a more prosperous yet sustainable future. Instead the battle will be won or lost by citizens, by us, on the streets of our cities.

The rise of cities marks a very different approach in how we will reach a new equilibrium. Our future will be invented piecemeal by different communities in multiple cities, as it cannot be conceived or implemented as a unitary plan. We celebrate some of the citizens in cities around the world who are already thinking differently and reinventing new ways to prosper that will last.

As modern societies steer away from government and towards governance, and from hierarchical control to networks, influence is inexorably shifting to citizens. The localism of our time is not narrow-minded parochialism or insular thinking: it is connected and emergent. What follows is a citizen's guide to direct this newfound energy.

R.C.
Windsor

Telling Stories

AGE OF HUMANS

For better or for worse the Earth will never be the same. We are transforming our home into a new and different planet. Human activities are increasing carbon dioxide levels in the atmosphere and nitrogen levels in the biosphere. Man-made chemicals are warming the climate, changing nutrient cycles and entering the food chain. Oceans are becoming more acidic and sea levels are rising. One third of all available fresh water has been diverted. Two-fifths of the entire land surface is used for planting and grazing. Fertile topsoil is eroding and may even vanish entirely. Earth's sixth mass extinction event is underway with the decimation of the only assortment of life known in the universe. Increasingly the sense of loss and the harmful effects of these massive changes are impinging on our daily lives, making them harder to ignore. However, despite our home becoming less hospitable, this is not a story about what we have lost. The time for grieving has passed.

We now live in a geological age where human impact on the planet is so significant that a new epoch, the Anthropocene or "Age of Humans", has been declared. To define a new geological epoch, a "golden spike" must be found in the deposits of the geological record globally. When a meteorite collided with Earth some sixty-six million years ago, huge amounts of the metal iridium were dispersed across the globe. The golden spike in iridium deposits can now be seen in the geological strata marking the end of the Cretaceous epoch and with it the mass death of all non-avian dinosaurs.

The story of the human race will be told in the geological record. The golden spike that will mark the Anthropocene in the future geological record is currently up for debate. The shortlist includes the radioactive sediments from nuclear bomb tests blown into the stratosphere before settling down in the soil; the unburned carbon spheres emitted by coal-fired power stations around the world that has left a permanent trace in sediment and glacial ice; and the prolific plastic pollution that will leave behind micro-plastic particles in fossils. It doesn't really matter which markers will outlast us: we are already living through the end of the world as we know it.

Climate change is one of the more profound and harmful man-made transformations. It is difficult to grasp the magnitude of our collective impact, as the measurements are so far removed from any human scale that we can understand. A couple of analogies may help to convey the thinness of the atmosphere and the staggering rate of heat building up. If you could drive straight up in a car at highway speeds, you would be in outer space in under an hour. That's a small enough distance that most can relate to: many people have longer daily commutes to work, each way. Beyond this thin layer of atmosphere is nothing but cold, dark space. The atmosphere seems vast as we look up at it from below but you would pass through it very quickly if you were not held down by gravity.

Within this thin shell, the heat build-up from man-made global warming is equivalent to exploding four hundred thousand Hiroshima atomic bombs per day. It is simply impossible to draw an analogy between the extra energy Earth is gaining each day from 250 trillion watts (joules per second) and anything that is remotely comprehensible. The energy released by one atomic bomb is shocking in the scale of its destruction. The energy released by two atomic bombs was enough to lead to the end of a world war.

How do we begin to imagine the energy equivalent to releasing four hundred thousand atomic bombs every day? It is obvious enough to do the maths and see that one very large quantity of energy does not go into one relatively thin layer of atmosphere. Certainly humans do seem tiny compared to the atmosphere and oceans, but *en masse* we have an impact that is beyond even our vast imagination.

It is commonplace to defer to the conclusions of experts across a range of subjects, as we clearly do not have the capacity to learn about everything. We do this all the time in our daily lives, visiting doctors when we are ill or listening to weather forecasts to find out when it will rain. The same is true of climate change: most people defer to the expert consensus of climate scientists for an informed opinion about something far more complicated than predicting the weather. In turn, scientists need to support their opinions with research findings and hard data, and are subjected to a critical peer-review process.

A survey of all (over twelve thousand) peer-reviewed abstracts on the subject "global climate change" and "global warming" published between 1991 and 2011 found that over ninety-seven percent of the papers agreed with the position that humans are causing global warming. A further review in 2016 by John Cook et al. across different scientists' surveys on climate change concluded that the finding of ninety-seven percent consensus in published climate research is robust and consistent. As far as the science goes (if it is happening and if we are the cause) the debate is closed. When it comes to our humanity (if we care enough to change our behaviour) the debate is wide open. Highlighting this agreement over the facts but disagreement on the response serves not as a denunciation, but as a cry for you to take action.

Equally disturbing is the loss of biodiversity, a phrase that sanitises the spectre of mass extinction. It takes millions of years for life to recover from a mass extinction. The overwhelming cause of this loss of life is humankind, wilfully from poaching and blindly from the destruction of habitats, overpopulation and pollution. The most deadly aspect of human activity is the speed of our impact that simply gives other species no time to adapt.

One quarter of all mammals and one third of all amphibians are threatened today with extinction. Every species we wipe out represents an irreversible loss to all future generations. If that was not momentous enough, diversity of plant and animal life plays a pivotal role in maintaining healthy ecosystems, and their absence inevitably endangers our own livelihood.

A lost whale becomes stranded in the River Thames in London, and dies after a massive rescue attempt to save its life. An orphan baby kangaroo is rescued in a Sydney suburb, from the pouch of its dead mother on the roadside. A five-day-old tamarin monkey is brought to a rescue centre in Bogota, because a man couldn't bring himself to leave the abandoned baby to die. A single death is a tragedy; a million deaths is a statistic. These words have been attributed to the Soviet leader Joseph Stalin, and ring true for all the individuals of a species that is dying out. Somehow we need to remind ourselves that mass extinction is not just a statistic.

Climate change plays its part in devastating the web of life. At the same time this web is fundamental to natural solutions for absorbing greenhouse gases, such as photosynthesis by green plants. We cannot reduce biodiversity loss without mitigating climate change, and we cannot mitigate climate change without reducing biodiversity loss. The two are interwoven. Climate change is no more important or profound than mass extinction; it is just that the sense of crisis is greater because we feel the impact in everyday life.

Sadly, the average person has not heard of many of the flora and fauna that are endangered, and countless species will probably disappear before scientists even manage to identify them. The known unknown of climate change is more tangible to us than the unknown unknown of losing untold species. We have at last woken up to climate change, and seen that our beds are burning. We need to feel the same sense of urgency about halting the decimation of life and realising that our future is tied to theirs.

Despite being very real, the changing state of the climate and decline of natural systems remain a remote concern. Basic needs are more pressing for many: over a billion people live without electricity and more than twice as many do not have access to clean water and sanitation. If it is a forced choice between meeting their immediate needs and addressing the longer-term harm inflicted on the environment, millions will understandably choose to improve their circumstances.

By the end of this century there will likely be more than ten billion people living on Earth, adding even more pressure to daily living. How can everyone possibly enjoy a reasonable standard of living in a way that is sustainable? In the following chapters we will explore how it is possible if we put our minds to it and act locally.

Leadership counts at all levels, especially in cities where the potential solutions to an unsustainable economy and unstable environment are concentrated. If you cannot wait, then jump to the chapter on "Civic Revolution" where you will discover the beliefs that are cutting through the doubts, the imperatives we face today as a society, and the attitudes to civic life that will make the difference. You will see how different aspects of city life can be transformed and in turn transform our prospects.

For many people whose basic needs have been met, what may happen in the future feels remote and irrelevant, obscured by the distraction or stress of busy day-to-day lives. It is something more distant and less important than work, something to worry about once bills are paid or maybe later when the children have left home, something less pressing than potholes in the road or vandalism in the neighbourhood. How can you persuade people to put the future ahead of the present? The answer is that you don't have to; we are not prisoners of the past and the present. Authors John Tierney and Martin Seligman reference how the mind is already drawn to the future, not driven by the past:

Behavior, memory and perception can't be understood without appreciating the central role of prospection... Human culture —

our language, our division of labor, our knowledge, our laws and technology — is possible only because we can anticipate what fellow humans will do in the distant future. We make sacrifices today to earn rewards tomorrow, whether in this life or in the afterlife promised by so many religions.

There is a porous divide between what we do in the present and what we do now for the future. Today is yesterday's tomorrow. The task is not to bring the "distant" future closer to the present and thus create a greater sense of urgency, but instead to see that taking action now is the best hope we have for a better present as well as for a more prosperous future.

There is inevitable resistance to giving up any aspect of a privileged lifestyle or material wealth, regardless of whether it is hard earned or obtained by good fortune. Yet if everyone in the world consumed as much as the average American citizen in order to "live well", the Earth would only be able to sustain one quarter of the current human population, and global warming and biological annihilation would accelerate further. To make ends meet, do we really expect some people to downshift and reduce their standard of living to improve our overall quality of life? The question presupposes that it is a zero sum game with only winners and losers. In reality it is a false trade-off between personal lifestyle needs and collective life support needs. What is needed is a different narrative for prosperity that remains aspirational, is sustainable and has the potential to enrich all of us.

Stories are fundamental in shaping our collective imagination and influencing our behaviour. We take action when enough of us believe in the same narrative. For example, the social norms that enable us to cooperate with different people in large organisations, or to collaborate with work colleagues we hardly know, are not based on instinct or close friendships but instead on shared beliefs in a story about a common purpose or a company mission. To change the world around us, we must start by telling each other stories that are powerful enough to hold our imagination.

Today's stories about prosperity are so familiar to us that they take on the appearance of truths and immutability of the laws of nature: consumption drives the economy; economic progress goes hand-in-hand with advances in technology; the global economy must grow so everyone can benefit. None of these things are inherently true. Not one is a narrative of transition and hope about how we might escape our plight unscathed and still prosper. Not one challenges the hegemony of economic growth.

ENDLESS GROWTH

Endless growth of the global economy is a myth. How can it be otherwise if we must continuously deplete finite natural resources and pollute where we live in order to grow? Over four decades ago a think tank called the Club of Rome commissioned a prescient report on the "predicament of mankind". The members of the club include notable scientists, economists and former heads of state from around the world, and their aim was, and still is, to promote understanding of the global challenges facing humanity and propose solutions.

The researchers involved used leading-edge computing power at the Massachusetts Institute of Technology to build a dynamic model that would track the world's economy and its impact on the environment. The task was daunting. The project team ultimately identified five basic factors that limit growth worldwide: human population, agricultural production, depletion of non-renewable resources, industrialisation and pollution. They modelled data up to 1970 and then developed scenarios to the year 2100 based on economic growth projections and the corresponding resource usage and its environmental impact.

The resulting book published in 1972, *The Limits to Growth*, drew the startling conclusion that if the growth trends continued under a "business as usual" scenario, the limits to growth on the planet would be reached within the next one hundred years and the result would be a sudden and uncontrollable decline in population and industrial capacity. By implication, this self-inflicted harm would result not only in the collapse of the human population but also in the collateral death of other species.

The report went on to say that we could alter this outcome and instead establish a state of sustainable ecological and economic stability. Global equilibrium was possible, satisfying the basic material needs of each person on Earth and providing each person with an equal opportunity to realise his or her individual human potential. They claimed that if we decided to strive for such a state of stable equilibrium, the sooner we began work to attain it the greater our chances of success.

Fast-forward fifty years, and the world is still tracking closely to *The Limits to Growth* "business-as-usual" scenario. We are in a hole and the equilibrium we have chosen is to keep on digging. The human population has grown steeply, industrial output and food consumption per capita have continued to rise, resources have been rapidly depleted and pollution is pervasive. Obligingly, thousands of species have died.

Even if we find additional natural resources such as new oil reserves, or invent alternative materials when other resources run out, we have not produced or found more natural "sinks" that can remove and store the substances we produce but no longer want. Earth's capacity to absorb the by-products and pollution from an expanding global economy is maxing out. It appears fatalistic to say we will exceed the limits of our ecosystem by continuing along the same insatiable path.

What is driving the continued pursuit of economic growth in spite of these facts? The answer is that not all facts are created equal. We choose to believe in a different story so ardently that it is assumed to be unquestionable fact – even though it was originally the figment of one Scotsman's imagination. The economist Adam Smith published *The Wealth of Nations* in 1776, during the first industrial revolution and in the same year as the American Declaration of Independence. His two-volume economics manifesto has become known as the Bible of Capitalism, which is ironic given the leaps of faith needed to believe his economic reasoning. Similar to the Bible, it is not known for its carefully constructed arguments but instead for the power of its stories that have since entered into the folklore of capitalism. Its influence rests not in Smith's ability to support his point of view with empirical evidence but in his skill as a consummate storyteller.

One of his most revolutionary and enduring tales is that increasing the profit of private entrepreneurs is the basis for increasing collective wealth and prosperity. In his words, the tale we believe in is no more than this:

When the landlord or monied man has a greater revenue than what he judges sufficient to maintain his own family, he employs either the whole or a part of the surplus in maintaining one or more menial servants. Increase this surplus, and he will naturally increase the number of those servants. When an independent workman, such as a weaver or shoemaker, has got more stock than what is sufficient to purchase the materials of his own work, he naturally employs one or more journeymen with the surplus, in order to make a profit by their work. Increase this surplus, and he will naturally increase the number of his journeymen.

The bold assumption behind Smith's imaginary examples of landlords and shoemakers is that rich individuals and private entrepreneurs will automatically use their profits to create more jobs and hire new employees, rather than spend their money on more luxuries for themselves. In Smith's story time, these landlords and shoemakers did not have the choice or temptation to spend their profits instead on a bigger car, an outdoor pool or holidays abroad.

In today's world with increasing automation and production efficiencies beyond Smith's imagination, our modern-day manufacturers need to produce more and more stuff that people don't need to support the employment of fewer and fewer people. With broken logic, Smith told us that more economic growth will result in more profit and more profit will inevitably benefit more people. The corollary is that increased consumption will drive economic growth that will increase further consumption, until this logic also spirals out of control.

Another powerful economic myth is based on an "invisible hand" that guides competing participants in a free-market economy who are driven by their own needs to unwittingly benefit society at large. Smith imagined that if people were allowed to trade freely without regulations or restrictions imposed by the government, self-interested traders would compete for buyers and the result naturally would be the best seller closing the deal and the buyer receiving better goods at the best price. Sounds familiar?

Smith's invisible hand became one of the primary justifications for an economic system of free-market capitalism that reigns supreme today. Our widely held belief is that whenever enough people demand something, the market will supply it and everyone will be happy. An economist who lived over two hundred years ago at a time when the first industrial revolution was barely in its infancy could scarcely have imagined the consequences for our society today.

The global economy grows because of our trust in such myths, and the actions we take as a result of them. In controlled economies without free markets, growth is pushed in order to catch up or to overtake. However, there is a fundamental flaw when growth itself becomes a supreme good, unrestricted by ethical or environmental considerations. Even if we put such restrictions aside, the plot will surely unravel, as endless growth is unattainable. However, we choose to believe that technology will save the day instead of overturning an intractable narrative.

TECHNOLOGY WILL SAVE THE DAY

We have a chronic habit of expecting technology to solve non-technical problems, from obesity (let's use sensors to help consumers track their activity levels) to education equality (let's have iPads in the classroom) to climate change (let's suck carbon dioxide out of the air). This dependency is borne from our ability to invent new capabilities for machines to help us do more. These technological inventions have kept the economy growing throughout the modern era, from the advent of mechanisation in the first industrial revolution to the pervasive power of digitisation and information technology today.

In August 2018, computing and mobile phone giant Apple became the world's first trillion-dollar public company, as a rise in its share price pushed it past this landmark valuation. The tech industry as a whole has grown exponentially as the amount of computing power we can squeeze into ever smaller devices has increased every year for the last five decades. Back in 1965, co-founder of microchip company Intel, Gordon Moore, predicted that chipmakers would be able to double the number of transistors on a chip roughly every twelve months. This exponential prediction in computing power known as "Moore's Law" has been proven correct, time and again, and is responsible for most of the advances in the digital age, from early mainframes to supercomputers. It has been used reliably in the semiconductor industry to set research and development targets for decades.

Let us pause for a moment to grasp the enormity of this phenomenon by recounting an old fable that has nothing to do with technology and everything to do with exponential growth. According to Indian legend, the tradition of serving *paal paysam* to visiting pilgrims started after a game of chess between the king and Lord Krishna himself. The king loved playing chess and would challenge wise visitors to a game. One day the king challenged a travelling sage and offered him any reward if the sage won. The sage modestly asked for a few grains of rice in the following manner: just one grain of rice on the first square of the chessboard, double that number of grains on the second square, and so on for each square on the board.

Having lost the game, the king honoured his word and ordered a bag of rice to be brought to the chessboard. Then he started placing rice grains according to the agreement: one grain on the first square, two on the second, four on the third... The king soon realised that he did not have enough rice to fulfil his promise. On the twentieth square he would have to put one million grains of rice; finally on the sixty-fourth square the king would have to place more than 18,000,000,000,000,000,000 grains of rice, about 210 billion tons, equivalent to covering the whole of India in a metre-thick layer of rice. At this point the sage revealed his true identity as Lord Krishna and told the king that he could pay the debt over time instead. To this day, visiting pilgrims are served *paal paysam*, as the king's debt has yet to be repaid.

Moore's prediction is not a law of physics; it is one of economics. According to a report sponsored by major semiconductor industries around the world, we will get to a point within the next five years when it will no longer be economically viable to make transistors smaller. Although Moore's Law is finally slowing down, other design approaches are taking over to achieve yet more efficiency gains and calculating speeds. This sustained increase in computing power has had such a big impact on our psyche that we presume technology in general will continue improving dramatically and that its future capabilities will solve ever more complex and non-technological problems.

There are two natural limits we expect technology to overcome for the global economy to continue its relentless growth. The first limit is the more obvious one: we are depleting natural resources such as fossil fuels faster than they can be replenished. The glib tech solution is to develop new ways of extracting reserves that are harder to reach, for example by fracking for oil and gas or by deep-water drilling. Aside from the controversies of these practices, consider the outcome of successfully extracting these reserves by using more advanced technology. The current reserves of all the fossil fuels companies – the oil, gas and coal deposits they have already claimed for future extraction – represent potential future emissions of 2,795 gigatons of carbon dioxide. One gigaton is equivalent to one billion (1,000,000,000) metric tons, if you can wrap your mind around such a gargantuan figure.

Here's the rub: research by the Potsdam Institute calculates that to reduce the risk of exceeding two degrees Celsius global warming to a one-in-five chance, the maximum future emissions over the forty years from 2010 to 2050 are 565 gigatons of carbon dioxide. This is our "carbon budget" – the maximum amount of carbon that can be released into the atmosphere while keeping a reasonable chance of staying below a two degrees Celsius temperature rise. As Bill McKibben, founder of 350.org, points out:

The thing to notice is 2,795 is five times 565. It's not even close. What those numbers mean is quite simple. This industry [oil and gas] has announced, in filings to the SEC and in promises to shareholders, that they're determined to burn five times more fossil fuel than the planet's atmosphere can begin to absorb.

For our own safety, most of the fossil fuel reserves banked by oil and gas companies should remain underground and not be extracted and burned in the future. The solution is not new extraction technologies but new regulations and alternatives. The energy companies have little financial incentive to lead this change in any meaningful way while we continue to credit these reserves on their books as assets worth trillions of dollars. What should be the financial value of these reserves if they are to be left in the ground?

The second natural limit is more insidious: we are creating pollution such as carbon dioxide faster than nature's absorptive capacity can handle. Some of the more grandiose technical solutions to this problem involve intervening in the Earth's natural systems on a large enough scale to counteract the effects of our unwanted by-products. Such geoengineering methods include reflecting more sunlight back into space to cool down our man-made warming or creating more "sinks" to absorb our toxins.

A growing number of scientists are convinced that it is time to start conducting geoengineering experiments. Researchers from a list of impressive universities that include Oxford and Cambridge, U.S. Ivy League schools and Indian Institutes of Technology are looking into what might work. The Royal Society, the U.K.'s science academy, has argued that geoengineering could prove useful in augmenting efforts to mitigate climate change and so should be the subject of more detailed research and analysis. Under consideration are geoengineering interventions where ironically we would pump even more substances into the environment to improve the absorption of other substances.

One big idea is "solar radiation management" that would have us inject sulphide gases into the atmosphere to block sunlight. The idea of using sulphate aerosols to offset climate warming is not new and was initially proposed in the mid-1970s. Now solar radiation management is the subject of hundreds of research papers by scientists using computer models to predict its consequences. The plan is straightforward: spray a mist of sulphuric acid into the lower stratosphere from planes flying above typical cruising altitudes; the sulphate aerosols formed are swept upwards by natural wind patterns and dispersed over the globe including the poles. Once spread across the stratosphere, these aerosols will reflect about one percent of the sunlight back into space and offset some of the warming effects below. According to proponents, this method would counter climatic changes, take effect rapidly, have low implementation costs and be reversible.

So what's not to like about this new tech solution? Some of the potential downsides include depletion of ozone that acts as our natural atmospheric protection against the sun's ultra-violet radiation; reduction in water precipitation around the world; and potential health effects from tons of sulphate particles returning into the lower atmosphere. In addition, there are significant ethical and political consequences of injecting sulphide gases into the stratosphere that become unevenly dispersed and hence disproportionately impact some countries more than others.

Since Earth is really an ocean planet, a second geoengineering idea is to increase the capacity of the oceans as a sink for absorbing more atmospheric carbon, by "fertilising" the oceans with tons of iron or other nutrients to stimulate plankton blooms. These organisms pull carbon out of the atmosphere and become deposited in the deep ocean when they die. Researchers worldwide have conducted thirteen major iron-fertilisation experiments in the open ocean since 1990, until the U.N. Convention on Biological Diversity put in place a moratorium on all ocean-fertilisation projects (apart from a loophole permitting smaller trials in coastal waters). This moratorium was in response to concerns about the adverse effects of these experiments, such as massive toxic algal blooms. Aside from the immediate toxicity, the unintended impacts of ocean fertilisation may be so far removed in distance and time from the initial sites where these interventions take place that it is extremely challenging to quantify the amount of carbon removed with any acceptable accuracy.

Conducting geoengineering experiments as the basis for full-scale implementation is a fundamentally flawed approach to assessing risk or validating effectiveness. The impact of this technology is simply untestable on a small scale, as Martin Bunzl, Director of the Rutgers Initiative on Climate and Social Policy, points out:

You can test a vaccine on one person, putting that person at risk, without putting everyone else at risk. So even though we have a lot of planetary wide goals – like eradicating smallpox – we can test them for untoward effects before full-scale implementation. Not so for geoengineering. You can't build a scale model of the atmosphere or tent off part of the atmosphere. As such you are stuck going directly from a model to full-scale planetary wide implementation.

Even if we could partition the atmosphere for test purposes, the evolving nature of our ecosystem makes predictions from experiments impossible. In the words of microbiologist Sallie Chisholm at the Massachusetts Institute of Technology:

Proponents of research on geoengineering simply keep ignoring the fact that the biosphere is a player (not just a responder) in whatever we do, and its trajectory cannot be predicted. It is a living breathing collection of organisms (mostly microorganisms) that are evolving every second—a 'self-organizing, complex, adaptive system' (the strict term). These types of systems have emergent properties that simply cannot be predicted. We all know this!

Yet proponents of geoengineering research leave that out of the discussion.

When it comes to deployment of geoengineering technology, technical considerations are no more important than social, legal, ethical and political concerns. Such concerns may yet be our best form of defence against such experimentation. These large-scale technical interventions are not mere distractions from solving the root cause, but are what economists call a "moral hazard" whereby we take unacceptable levels of risk because we believe we are protected (and that others will incur the cost). The moral hazard of our belief that technology will save the day is that we willingly incur more risk by not cutting emissions now, as we believe a future geoengineering solution will protect us and our children from the consequences of our inaction.

The alternative approach to coping with risk is based on the precautionary principle: when human activities, such as geoengineering, lead to morally unacceptable harm that is scientifically plausible but uncertain, actions should be taken to avoid or diminish that harm. Lack of evidence of harm is not the same thing as evidence of lack of harm!

No matter where we live, we can go outside on a clear night and look up into the sky, and wonder about what is out there. Famed cosmologist Stephen Hawking predicted that the human race only has one hundred years remaining to colonise another planet and avoid such hazards as overdue epidemics and climate change. Captivated by the story of colonising space, NASA, Mars One and SpaceX all intend to send people to Mars sometime in the 2030s. Mars One is planning a one-way trip for one hundred selected colonists to the red planet by the year 2026. The hardware for this mission needs to be designed, built, and tested extensively, but the technology exists, according to the company. There is a lot for technology to solve, from landing heavy cargo on the planet to creating habitats that have electricity, sanitation, clean air, potable water and food supplies. It's pioneering stuff that we can get really excited about.

What would this new home from home feel like? It would be a lot colder (the average temperature is minus sixty degrees Celsius). You can't breathe if you step outside (the atmosphere is ninety-five percent carbon dioxide). You would have to dig a long way to find any water (it is frozen and buried somewhere under the surface). Local weather is extreme (dust storms are capable of blanketing the entire planet and lasting for months). If these are the inhuman conditions on Mars, is it really easier and more desirable for a few to live in this extreme environment than to protect our more hospitable climate on Earth for everyone else?

A "moonshot" is an ambitious, pioneering tech project. The term originates from a speech by President John F. Kennedy in 1962 when he made the bold statement that Americans would go to the moon before the end of the decade; he believed it, and his vision came true on 20 July 1969. These days, the likes of Alphabet's research and development arm (formerly known as Google X) are seeking technology solutions to some of society's bigger problems such as climate change. According to its director, there are three components to a moonshot:

The first is, there has to be a huge problem with the world that we want to solve. The second is that there has to be some science-fiction sounding product or service that, if we could make it, however unlikely that is, would actually make that problem go away. And then there has to be some technology breakthrough that gives us some faith that we could actually at least get started on trying to build that product or service.

Solar radiation management, ocean fertilisation and colonising Mars all fall under this exciting moonshot thinking. But what if these ideas are missing the mark because taking action on climate change is not fundamentally a technical problem? We can figuratively reach for the moon with any daring project that has enough ambition. What if the moonshot thinking we really need does not require a science-fiction sounding product or service or even a moon, but instead needs a more human narrative with such power that it upends the myths locking in our current behaviour?

A NEW NARRATIVE

The difficulty lies not in telling a new story but in convincing everyone to believe it. Whenever there is a contradiction with the familiar stories that shape our world, the force of convention gives the established norm a big advantage. As creatures of habit, the more we do something the more likely we are to do it. A jolt in momentum and in our mindset is needed if we are to change our habits.

We have become caught in a trap of our own making. Those things that meet our needs for survival and health, for food and basic comfort, have been widely available for a long time in countless local areas that are economically advantaged. The advent of mass production devoted to these same basic goods has simply brought us the luxury of choice. This myriad is compounded by new luxuries that quickly become the necessities of life. Automobiles that once provided the luxury of mobility have become a necessity for our daily commutes. Luxuries such as smartphones, GPS navigators, espresso coffee machines and more, have been swallowed up in our pursuit of material satisfactions and have been turned into needs.

The phenomenon of this shift in our norms is termed the "shifting baseline syndrome", after researcher Daniel Pauly explained the idea in describing our relationship to the environment and the almost imperceptible shifts in our standards. The concept of our gradual accommodation to new norms is just as relevant to our insatiable consumer behaviour. We perceive products that are no longer new as normal and use them as our baseline against which we measure new. The same applies to services; for example, constant access to the internet is considered to be neither new nor a luxury but instead is accepted as the norm and has become a basic utility (a human right!) for everyone. Caught in this trap, we turn new luxuries into needs and then need new luxuries. We cannot escape because this is the nature of a way of life that is ordered by consumer myths.

In his book, *Sapiens*, Professor Harari argues that there are several factors preventing us from realising our lives are ordered by no more than myths. One reason why we do not see this order as imaginary is because it shapes the physical world around us. Western culture values individualism very highly, and this translates into modern houses divided into private rooms for individual family members, for example. Our hopes are also conditioned by these myths, so that it becomes almost impossible to differentiate between our own wishes and the aspirations of underlying myths. For instance, going on holiday abroad may be no more than consumerism pushing us to travel to different places and experience the world.

These shared beliefs are persistent because they remain after a single individual changes his or her mind, and even after they are contradicted by facts. The imagined order that the Earth is flat or that the Sun orbits the Earth was not easily dispelled despite the opposing evidence. The more recent myth that climate change is a natural phenomenon endures despite overwhelming facts and evidence to the contrary. To displace an existing imagined order, we must weave a new narrative into the physical world so that it captures the imagination and shapes the aspirations of enough people for us to take the collective leap.

And leap we must. We are forced to rethink the current order rather than remain within it, as our continuously expanding human system has burst its seams and overshot Earth's carrying capacity. In their research, Johan Rockstrom and an internationally renowned team identified nine "planetary boundaries" that we exceed at our peril. Specifically, we are vulnerable to increased global warming from climate change; to depleting the ozone layer that blocks the radiation from the sun; and to loading the atmosphere with aerosols that interfere with climate regimes and monsoon systems. We put ourselves at risk from increasing the acidity of the oceans until marine life collapses; from consuming our freshwater reserves until water becomes scarce; and from cutting down our forests until land use changes impoverish topsoil, biodiversity and water flows. We are endangered by our emissions of chemical pollutants; by changing the flows of nitrogen and phosphorus, which are essential for agricultural production; and by the loss of biodiversity.

Knowledge of these boundaries is vital but this knowledge may have limited impact in changing our behaviour. It does not provide solutions. Knowing there is a boundary we should not cross is often an invitation to get as close to the edge as we think we can go. We are quite capable of dispassionately quantifying these global limits, although we are not good judges at living within the boundaries we have identified. We have already overstepped four: atmospheric carbon dioxide levels (an indicator for climate change), the extinction rate (an indicator for loss of biodiversity), deforestation, and nitrogen and phosphorus flows. How much longer can we continue to exceed any one of these boundaries before large, irreversible changes become unavoidable? We don't really know.

The research team went further and singled out climate change and loss of biodiversity as the two core boundaries that are connected to all the rest. Either one could "drive the Earth system into a new state". Neither can be ignored and we will address both.

When we pause to reflect on the widespread harm we are causing, there are inevitable feelings of regret about what we are doing and perhaps a sense of fear of the unintended consequences. However, such emotions do not provide the energy we need to make change happen. In fact, behavioural research findings tell us that what is needed is a realistic message of hope. One review led by Professor Paschal Sheeran of 129 experimental studies that successfully changed attitudes and behaviours found that the least effective strategies involved inducing regret or arousing fear. Although it sounds like a platitude, effective change started with a positive message: we need constructive, worthwhile reasons for embracing the challenges we face.

In the political arena, Barack Obama understood this fundamental need for hope and its power for change when he burst onto the scene at the Democratic National Convention in 2004. At the convention he called for "hope in the face of difficulty, hope in the face of uncertainty, the audacity of hope... a belief in things not seen, a belief that there are better days ahead". He carried his message of hope into his presidential campaign, captured it succinctly in the slogan "Yes We Can", and captured a nation.

The predominant global economic model today is based on the myth of thriving by getting rich. If we take a breath and look up, it's not hard to see the hope that everyone can benefit from endless economic expansion is misplaced in a world of finite resources and boundaries. Instead, we need a better vision of hope than individual riches, and a safer path than continuous consumption to realise our aspirations.

The new narrative of hope has its roots in the place where you live. There will be different places in your life if you move around, but at each stage the sense of belonging to that place remains important. The cities and neighbourhoods where people have the strongest emotional attachments are the ones that have a distinctiveness about them. They remind us of where we are by their personality and by their public spaces, from Highbury in London to Harlem in New York. Conversely there is an emptiness about places that lack character, where Gertrude Stein once famously said, "there is no 'there' there".

Human habitat that comprises neighbourhoods, towns and cities is every bit as important to the environment as natural habitat. There is no sustainability without urban places that limit their environmental impacts. Urban theorist Mike Davis goes further, claiming:

There is no planetary shortage of 'carrying capacity' if we are willing to make democratic public space, rather than modular, private consumption, the engine of sustainable equality.

Davis appeals to the paradox that the single biggest cause of our planetary overshoot – the urbanisation of humanity – is potentially the principal solution to the problem of human survival. Cities are integral to the new narrative of growing deeper roots to address the challenges of the economy, equity and the environment. This sense of belonging is not simply an antidote to becoming citizens of nowhere, but the key to unlocking a sustainable future.

In the chapters that follow, we look beyond the role of nation states and see that cities are the places that have the greatest influence over life on Earth. We sift for clues in our past that help us navigate an unsustainable global economy and an unstable environment. We discover the beliefs we should hold if we are to chart a new course to prosperity; the imperatives we should heed if we are to stay the course; and the attitudes to civic life we should embrace if we are to steer the course in an alternative direction.

For the new narrative to be more than wishful thinking, the direction we take must be measurable and quantifiable. The sheer number of local initiatives we could pursue might suggest there is no simple or consistent approach. However, there is a coherent way forward and this guide identifies indicators we can turn to that are common to all cities in bringing this new narrative to life.

The first stage begins where we live, with us. We have always been citizens (in the literal sense, as inhabitants of a particular place) before we were branded consumers or defined by our work. Too many of us have forgotten about the importance of the connection with our city, connected instead to products or a profession. The term "city" is used throughout this book as shorthand for any place with a relatively high degree of urban-ness. It may not rest well with the purists that there is no exact definition or demarcation. In England and Wales, for example, a city was only a city in the past if there was a diocesan cathedral. In this book official city status is unimportant: it is the density and proximity of people that matters, not the absolute size of the city or presence of a cathedral.

If human civilisation and the global economy we have created are to thrive in the long run then both must be regenerative. The path outlined here is within our reach, although we will need different convictions about civic life and its importance. Sustainability is the outcome, although the aim is to fulfil our hope for a prosperous future that can last. This story makes no predictions: how the story ends depends on what we begin.

Rising Up

CULT OF BIGNESS

Every human life, society or organisation has its seasons. There are times for growing and acquisition and times for cutting back and simplification. Both should occur over the natural course of events and both are needed to achieve a balanced outcome. Too much growth or too little pruning invariably creates a problem later as scale and complexity overwhelm our ability to recognise and address the issues arising from excess. The problem is not growth itself but when growth has exceeded a safe scale and proportion. Determining when something is too big, and how to moderate growth before it turns into a crisis, is an art as much as a science, and became the life's work of the political thinker Leopold Kohr.

The decades that followed the Second World War were a period when military and political size became equated unquestioningly with power. During this period, Kohr undertook his formative research as a political scientist to understand why bigger nations collapse despite their power. Unfashionably, he challenged the prevailing Cold War dogma of bigger is better by questioning whether "the problem is not the thing that is big, but bigness itself".

This sharp insight gets lost when the political debate is framed as a binary choice between right and left, between neo-liberalism with its free-market society and socialism with its government interventions. One side or the other is always blamed for our contemporary ills. What if detractors on both sides of the argument are wrong? Kohr's radical claim is that our problems are not caused by a particular political system *per se*, but by building the system beyond the human scale where individuals can no longer play a meaningful role in the society that shapes their lives.

We see this manifested in the complex and long-distance problems that over-extended organisations face, both operationally and economically, that are simply beyond the ability of their employees, management or local governments to solve. No amount of market correction, governmental regulation or organisational change can compensate for the pace with which the problems of excessive size outdistance the efforts to catch up with them.

There is a natural limit to all organisations and forms of governance, a certain size and relative proportion that facilitate proper social, economic and civic functioning. Larger organisations may claim to be better because they are more diversified and have access to a greater pool of talent and financial resources. However, these advantages are more limited in scope and availability than is commonly perceived.

The fact that so many people today work for successful global corporations and other far-reaching organisations does not contradict the inherent weakness of their overreach. These entities have blind spots because of their bigness, and as a result they operate in ways that are detrimental to the world outside. The fault lines become ever more visible as they continue to grow beyond a human scale.

In his book *Politics*, the Ancient Greek philosopher Aristotle quantified this natural limit in the context of the optimum size of a city-state. In his view a community of citizens would function properly and remain cohesive if it did not exceed the "largest number that suffices for the purposes of life and can be taken in at a single view". To transpose this scale into a contemporary social network metric, it is helpful to consider the measure of social distance between people, or their "degree of separation". You are one degree away from everyone you know personally, and two degrees away from everyone they know. By this measure of connectivity, a community would not be too big if there were at most two degrees of separation between any two people within it.

If bigness itself is a problem, where has the pervasive myth come from that bigness is the driver of economic progress? Firstly, as you would expect, the power elite and fat cats who have benefited the most from extending their control within the current economic system are the most vocal proponents. Although these influential people represent a very small minority, others understandably feel relatively powerless in challenging them. Secondly, although the expansive growth of capitalism has undoubtedly improved the standard of living for billions of people, its true cost has not been accounted for. The social and environmental costs from large-scale industrialisation and planetary urbanisation, problems such as the rapid growth of informal settlements and pollution, have not been fully recognised. Hence judgement on the benefits of bigness has been too one-sided.

Criticism of untamed growth still remains unfashionable today because it continues to be a direct challenge to the narrative of the goodness of growth. Nonetheless, the global economic crises we have seen recently are caused not by too little growth but by too much. Driven by their appetite for risk, banks grew so large and interconnected prior to the financial crisis of 2008 they were deemed to be "too big to fail" and their collapse considered disastrous to the entire global economy. Instead of failing, these banks were bailed out with huge sums of public money. In the U.K. alone, the government committed to spending over one trillion dollars at various points between 2007 and 2011 on bailing out the banks. By March 2011, the figure was over seven hundred billion dollars, roughly equivalent to the entire Gross Domestic Product of Switzerland.

Of course there was another choice, as Michael Schuman reported in the midst of the U.S. bailout of its auto industry that was also entangled in the global financial crisis. In his article for *Time*, titled "Why Detroit is not too big to fail", he observed:

The experience in Asia over the past decade shows that no company is too big to fail, the fallout is often not as painful as the dire predictions and, in the medium to long term, economies may actually benefit by permitting their deadweight to die.

The experience in Asia that he was referring to was the collapse of the giant Korean company Daewoo in 1999, one of the country's four largest industrial corporations. There were about twenty divisions and almost three hundred subsidiaries within the sprawling conglomerate. Daewoo manufactured and sold everything from automobiles to ships, oil tankers and planes; had businesses in electronics, textiles, telecoms and financial services; and managed hotels and other properties around the world. This single corporation had over fifty billion dollars in revenues and accounted for over ten percent of the entire South Korean Gross Domestic Product.

Daewoo also had more than eighty billion dollars in debt and other liabilities, and if allowed to go bankrupt the failure would be catastrophic for the Korean banking sector and wider economy. Except it wasn't. Korea's economy didn't even stop growing. Gross Domestic Product grew over nine percent the year Daewoo failed and over eight percent the following year. The group was broken apart and its debt was restructured. Billions were lost as government officials and banks acknowledged the reality that Daewoo could not have paid back many of its loans. Nonetheless, the Korean economy ended up stronger without Daewoo as a multitude of smaller companies received investments that had previously been wasted in shoring up the enormous organisation. The fear that this corporate giant was too big to fail proved to be unfounded.

Another example of gigantism, in the political world, is the unified trade and monetary body of twenty-eight European Union member countries. Originally conceived as a bloc of six nations, its intent was to unite France and Germany economically and politically to secure a more lasting peace after the Second World War. Its aim was both honourable and practical, inspired by the Schuman Declaration:

The pooling of coal and steel production should immediately provide for the setting up of common foundations for economic development as a first step in the federation of Europe, and will change the destinies of those regions which have long been devoted to the manufacture of munitions of war, of which they have been the most constant victims. The solidarity in production thus established will make it plain that any war between France and Germany becomes not merely unthinkable but materially impossible.

Some forty years later, thanks to the Maastricht Treaty, what began as a production arrangement, primarily between two neighbours involving coal and steel, became the European Union. In turn this led to the creation of the single European currency launched in 1999, and by 2015 the enlarged Union had a total population of over five hundred million citizens.

The European Union has grown so big and unaccountable that it no longer works in the interests of all its individual members. The most recent and dramatic example is Greece that buckled under the deep differences between European economies. To avoid the humiliation of defaulting on its debts and being forced out of the single currency, Greece endured draconian measures imposed by Brussels and a biting austerity programme that prolonged the country's already harsh recession. The Greek tragedy is that an economic catastrophe on the scale of the Great Depression fell on a country that had been encouraged into the European Union, not because of the neglect of the bloc's governing body but under its direct supervision.

Given such rifts and resentment among European Union countries, there is little argument against the need for the gigantic Union to reform before it collapses under its own weight. Emmanuel Macron, the staunchly pro-European President of France, has said that time is running out for the

European Union to reinvent itself and to "give Europe back to its citizens". The U.K. chose not to wait or to participate, and in an act of unilateral political disarmament voted divisively to leave.

There is a remedy to this gigantism that is grounded in a more human scale. The rising will come from the influence of the smallest, not the biggest. And it starts by growing deeper roots where you live.

TREASURE ISLANDS

Where will a new kind of prosperity take hold that stands a chance of lasting? To answer this question and appreciate the strength of its connection, we must journey back in time to its origins. The word "city" originates from the Latin *civitas* but the concept of the city as a political entity came to us from the Ancient Greeks under the name of *polis*. The *polis* is the predecessor of concepts such as civic self-governance and citizenship, and many of the English words today associated with the process and structures of governance, from "politics" to "metropolitan", stem from this antiquity.

By 800 BC there were hundreds of these city-states, or *poleis*, in the Ancient Greek world. Typically a *polis* consisted of a single fortified city built on a harbour or huddled around a central defensible hill. A few *poleis* extended their territorial control with naval fleets, such as Athens and Rhodes, but most were small in size, concentrated, and isolated by surrounding mountains. All were independent political entities ruled by their citizens rather than by a king. Each was a focal point of social, political, cultural and religious life.

The Ancient Greeks believed that each city-state had its own unique and often mythical founder. The city of Athens, for example, was named after its patron deity Athena, the goddess of wisdom. Complete in itself, a *polis* also had its own foreign policy and even coinage. It followed naturally from all the different ways citizens interacted with one another and differentiated themselves that each *polis* was a tightly knit community and very personal place.

Famous Greek philosophers such as Aristotle and Plato thought that a *polis* should be of a size for every citizen to know everyone else, believing that if it were any bigger it would become too impersonal and not work for the benefit of each individual citizen. Social identity was strengthened through deliberate urban planning by creating communal gathering places for political discourse and spiritual celebrations as well as for artistic performances and athletic activities. Citizens would gather and mix on festival days, unique to the place and specific to the history of the *polis*. A common community history was further reinforced and commemorated in the public statues of local gods, leaders, benefactors and sporting champions.

Despite the bygone era and the small size of such city-states, their influence has been far-reaching. We look back to Athens, whose ancient city wall encompassed an area of less than two square kilometres, not simply to understand the Greeks but for the birth in the Western world of such things as drama and philosophy, architecture and democracy.

City-states were not just a Western construct for how people should live together. In China, the period of the Zhou Dynasty from 770 BC known as the "Spring and Autumn" period was the age of the city-state that lasted for three centuries. The basin of the Yellow River was home to hundreds of small states, each consisting of a single city and its immediate vicinity. Public life in each city-state was centred on political and religious sites and activities, with citizens routinely meeting in major squares and in the courtyards of ancestral temples to discuss political affairs and to assemble in times of crisis.

In contrast with Ancient Greece, little trace remains today of the civic power of the Chinese city-states. During the Spring and Autumn period, the continued presence of the Zhou Dynasty lessened civic development and independent thinking on self-government, with no radically new forms of authority created to replace the dynasty. At the same time the relatively minor role of the merchant class in these city-states inhibited more distinctive urban cultures and political autonomy.

Although Chinese civilisation during this period did not develop new political theories on self-governance, or institutions for greater participation in local government by citizens, the influence of city-states left a lasting legacy in the cultural development of philosophy and religion. The Spring and Autumn period is also known as the time of the "Hundred Schools of Thought", when the existence of so many city-states enabled many more new ideas to flourish and coexist. Major philosophies emerged that were passed to later empires: Confucianism, Legalism and Taoism. With its focus on ethical models of family and public interaction, Confucianism became the official imperial philosophy of China that went on to prevail during the dynasties that followed.

Fast-forward to the Renaissance period, and we see the history of Italy is the history of cities. Whereas the modern nation state of Italy has been around for just over 150 years, powerful city-states existed in the region for centuries and were the domains of some of the largest and richest places in Europe. Some of these city-states gained so much economic and political prominence that by the time of the Renaissance they were recognised and treated as independent powers on the European stage. Today, the Italian city-states of the fourteenth and fifteenth centuries are acknowledged for their impact in the development of Western political, economic, artistic and literary customs.

Why did these city-states become so powerful? In the Middle Ages, the northern half of the Italian peninsula was one of the most urbanised areas in Europe, with around thirty percent of the population living in cities. The endless demands by the Holy Roman Emperor and the papacy for military and financial support exhausted many of these city dwellers and their city's coffers, prompting their fight for autonomy. City-states emerged as a result, and no longer bound to the emperor or the pope as the highest governing authority, they turned away from prerogative powers towards a new form of city governance that belonged to the people.

Civic administrators and thinkers developed new political theories promoting the idea that self-governance was the nexus between prosperity and thriving communities. City rule by the people for the people became the new narrative that inspired people's collective imagination and actions. Sassoferrato, a prominent Italian law professor in the fourteenth century, proclaimed that although kings were rulers of their kingdoms, the city was its own ruler, beholden to none other than its residents.

The moral, social and political philosophy that today is known as "civic humanism" emerged during this period and most notably from Florence. The humanistic scholars adopted the ideal of an active civic life in the service of the state, with thought-leaders putting theory into practice by holding important civic posts. One of the more prominent was the Chancellor of Florence, who espoused the principles of republican self-government in his letters to other city-states as the common cause that united all free cities against aggression or subjugation.

Inspired by an infectious civic renaissance, cities developed legal and administrative frameworks to reinforce their powers and those of an emerging urban merchant class. Dependency on the traditional power of the landed nobility was eclipsed by the fortunes of commerce and banking. Public affluence grew immeasurably from this civic revival as art and architecture flourished. The economic prosperity of these cities enabled them to assume responsibility for great public building projects such as cathedrals, libraries and *palazzi*. Such undertakings not only proclaimed each city's greatness but also how great it was to be a resident of that city.

If these European city-states were so powerful politically and successful commercially, what happened to them? In short, they became victims of the most destructive conflict in Europe before the twentieth-century world wars, a conflict known subsequently as the Thirty Years' War (1618–48). By the early seventeenth century, most of continental Europe was in a state of total war. Fighting had escalated from the Holy Roman Empire's attempts to impose Roman Catholicism across its domain, into a widening series of military campaigns and alliances that dragged central Europe into conflict over religious and territorial disputes.

The chaos ensnared all the major European powers, from the Holy Roman Empire to the House of Savoy to the German princes to the national armies of France, Spain, Denmark and Sweden, to roving bands of mercenaries. As the war evolved, it became less about religion and more about which powers would ultimately govern Europe. Many of the contending armies plundered as they criss-crossed through Europe, leaving behind ravaged city-states and ruined towns.

The Thirty Years' War claimed at least four million lives, with some estimates as high as twelve million. Overall the population of Europe fell by a staggering twenty percent, with some areas reduced by as much as sixty percent. The war finally ended in a series of peace treaties known as the Peace of Westphalia. Out of fear of a resurgence of fighting and the horror and depravity of war, the parties were desperate to enshrine a way to hold back aggression from all directions and to keep a balance of power. The treaties created the basis for national self-determination and protection, recognising the exclusive right of each party over its respective lands and people, as well as the right to determine its own religion.

Multiple territorial adjustments consolidated rights on the ground with buffer zones and clearly defined borders for security. Each state had sovereignty over its territory and its domestic affairs, and each state was equal in international law no matter its size. This principle of equality and non-interference in another state's domestic affairs established a new system of political order in Europe based on the concept of coexisting sovereign states. Thus emerged from the Peace of Westphalia the idea of the modern system of territorial states, in contrast to former city-states that did not have sufficient land to buffer potential ground attacks. As European influence extended across the globe through a combination of trade and colonisation, this concept of territories instead of cities as sovereign states became central to world order and international law.

The modern nation state is a specific form of sovereign state, guided by a cultural identity (a nation) and hence is not only a political structure based on a territory but also an ingrained cultural entity. The spread of this national idea was aided by developments in mass society, notably mass literacy and the mass media, which were well underway by 1800. Nationalism became the ideal in France during the Revolution and was used to legitimise the sovereignty of the state. This ideal spread through Europe and later the rest of the world. Island nations such as Britain, Japan and Iceland became nation states through circumstance, as their insular territory meant natural limits of state and nation coincided.

Nation states have typically grown from states rather than from nations. In most cases states already existed as territories that were controlled by royalty and their armies. Over time, rulers sought to create a sense of national identity within their state in order to corral the people's loyalty and legitimise their rule. China and India are examples of states that have developed genuine national identities over time as a result of the common history and experience of their respective citizens and the reforms that have given their citizens varying degrees of representation.

Borders between nation states have also created frontlines for ethnic or religious clashes. The conflict between India and Pakistan over Kashmir, for example, has endured for over seventy years, starting in 1947 when the Indian subcontinent was split into a predominantly Hindu India and a Muslim Pakistan. Kashmir was free to accede to either nation, and its accession to India sparked a military dispute that continues to this day. In Africa, colonial borders drawn arbitrarily across the continent by Europeans created artificial states that had no regard for people's heritage or cultural claims to the land. Top-down imposition of contrived nationalism by some African rulers only added to ethnic tensions within territories characterised by fragmented cultural identities.

One example of a young nation that built its own state is none other than the United States of America. In the eighteenth century there were thirteen British colonies in North America with a unified sense of American culture borne from the commerce and migration between them. Newspapers, roads and a postal system increased the exchange of common ideas and products. The resentment of the Americans towards the British grew with increasing taxation by a distant U.K. parliament to which they elected no representatives. At the same time companies like the British East India Company brewed further unrest by monopolising tea and other commodities.

Eventually most Americans joined the cause for independence and succeeded in overthrowing British rule. Having reached melting point, America's Founding Fathers created a Constitution for the new nation state that united the people (who were not slaves) across a single territory and empowered them with certain unalienable rights. The metaphor of a "melting pot" evolved to define Americans of all different backgrounds by their shared values, stirring America's willingness to accommodate difference in the spirit of an aspirational nation state.

In truth, the idea of a "nation state" is more of an ideal than a reality as there are very few territories where a single ethnic, religious or culturally homogeneous population resides. Instead, diversity, and its potential benefits, is even more pronounced in our pluralistic era that is shaped by globalisation and the dispersion of people of different cultural identities across the world. Nonetheless, the concept of nation states has superseded the historical self-governing practices of city-states. A few city-states still remain today in various guises. The Vatican is the smallest independent city-state in the world and is a tiny remnant of the extensive Papal States that were dissolved in the mid-nineteenth century. Almost all of its population is made up of priests and nuns from around the world.

The city-state of Monaco is little more than a headland that extends into the Mediterranean Sea near the French-Italian border. It is a resort, really the dream of Prince Rainier III who ruled it from 1949, and is a relic from Medieval Europe that was allowed to survive by its more powerful neighbours. Cities like Dubai and Abu Dhabi enjoy such a high degree of autonomy that they function as city-states within the context of their sovereign state, the United Arab Emirates. In China, Macau and Hong Kong also behave in this way, and today Hong Kong is the world's most populous city-state with over seven million citizens.

Rivalling Hong Kong is Singapore, an island city-state and global hub for commerce, finance, shipping and travel. Looking down on its glittering city skyline from the infinity pool on the fifty-seventh floor of the Marina Bay Sands hotel, the view is futuristic and green. Gardens by the Bay stretches out below, built as part of the city-state's vision to become a "city in a garden". These public gardens include conservatories, waterways, aerial bridges and superstructures clad in living plants, and focus people's attention on enhancing civic life by improving biodiversity within the city.

The population of Singapore is diverse, with a Chinese majority and substantial minorities of Malays and Indians. Singaporeans fill the streets, yet traffic flows smoothly and there is very little crime. The city-state consistently ranks towards the top on urban quality of life measures and on human development indicators such as life expectancy and income per person. Ruled by one party that is legitimised at the polls, the heavily regulated status quo is set to continue, as there are no drastically different views on national issues for alternative parties to uphold and virtually no official corruption that would undermine the party's power.

Is Singapore the exception or a sign of things to come? Most people would consider nation states to be the inevitable shape of how society is organised physically and politically, as this is all we have known. But these constructs are a relatively recent phenomenon and we don't need to delve into the distant past to see the alternative of city-states in action today. Nation states will not disappear from the map but the relative power of cities both large and small is rising once again. Cities, not territories, will be the wellspring of a new kind of prosperity.

REBIRTH OF CITY-STATES

Will we see the resurgence of city-states? The city-states of the twenty-first century will not be as insular as their predecessors since they coexist in a world of nation states and a world wide web, but they will function in an increasingly self-reliant way for the benefit of their residents. Modern cities have dual nationalities based on a civic sense of citizenship derived from their physical communities and locations, and on a cultural sense of nationhood derived from a more imaginary community at national level.

This duality is a variable relationship, with the emphasis changing over time, from its civic duties to its wider role within the nation. The sense of cities belonging to a nation state has been dominant for the last two centuries. Cities will remain beholden, but in this century they will turn decisively to the other pole of their dual nationality as their civic powers grow.

This shift in outlook by cities from participant to protagonist is propelled by three nearly irreversible phenomena working in unison: urbanisation, devolution and empowerment. Increasing urbanisation is projected to continue well into this century as a product of more births in urban areas and the sustained migration of people from rural surroundings. The megatrend is worldwide, with Africa leading the way as the most rapidly urbanising continent. The urban shift has been so substantial that despite a decrease in the proportion of people living in informal settlements around the world, the absolute number of people living in such conditions has continued to increase. Rapidly growing cities in these regions are becoming powerhouses by virtue of their increasing urban population, but face this persistent challenge of integrating large minorities of underserved residents.

Beyond the sheer increase in numbers of city dwellers, devolution is the second megatrend that strengthens civic power. In Europe, for example, Austria, Belgium, Germany and Switzerland are staunchly federal; Italy is on the path to federalisation; France and Spain are highly decentralised; the U.K. and Portugal have transferred considerable powers to their regions; Poland is poised to follow. As the United Nations noted in its *World City Report 2016*, what is most astonishing is how so many states around the world are moving in the same direction:

As cities grow, and spread out over the land, they have been the recipients of a worldwide trend to devolve power from the national to the local level... The fact that so many states have chosen to move along the path of decentralization constitutes a remarkable phenomenon.

Devolution of power and funding, from national to civic governments, is widely recognised as a more effective way to tailor policies to local needs, contributing to increased dynamism by creating opportunities for local innovation. It is the preferred mechanism to increase local participation and accountability. More cities are experiencing the effects of less centralised governance and embracing decision-making at the local level. However, decentralisation works only when the resource-raising powers that are granted are commensurate with the newfound civic responsibilities. As a result, central governments will continue to face pressure to relinquish more financial control over municipalities as the balance of power shifts.

The third megatrend is city empowerment. Although devolution and empowerment appear to be two sides of the same coin, the actions taken by cities and citizens with their newfound powers are different from devolved national policies. One example of this profound change is the way in which cities and citizens are beginning to buy, and increasingly to produce, energy to meet their immediate needs. Decentralised energy generation at the municipal level enables cities and their residents to become producers. The motivation is part financial and part empowerment. As we shall see later, citizens in some cities have regained autonomy and self-determination over one of their essential needs – energy. This empowerment paradigm, of which energy supply is one important element, points to a future where citizens keep as many urban life support systems as possible within their direct control.

Cities matter because they are large economies in themselves. In a report on cities and climate change, the World Bank looked at the combined clout of the fifty largest cities in the world. In total, the Gross Domestic Product of these cities ranked second in the world compared with countries, ahead of such states as China, Japan, India, Germany and Russia. Together, these fifty cities also emitted more greenhouse gases than any other nation state in the world except the USA and China.

No doubt cities are part of the problem. By the same token they are part of the solution. Dense urban areas have the potential to provide a high-quality, low-carbon way of life in the most efficient way. For example, New York City is one of the world's biggest greenhouse gas emitters, but on a per capita basis the city's emissions are much lower than other large U.S. cities. New York City is not unique in this aspect: research conducted for the World Bank Group calculated that an average city household in forty-eight major U.S. metropolitan areas generates up to thirty-five percent less greenhouse gas emissions than in the corresponding suburb.

Although nation states have bigger economies than their cities, they have to contend with the uneven economic impact of globalisation at home and its failure to deliver prosperity for all. For globalisation to succeed in a world of nation states it needs to retain their support, and the nation states themselves need to accept reductions in their sovereignty for the greater global good. There lies the inevitable tension between what might be considered to be in the sovereign national interest and in the wider global interest. To a large extent, cities sidestep the issue, as globalisation is not so much a challenge to their sovereignty as an opportunity for increased connectivity.

In a 2016 TED talk, global strategist Parag Khanna compared the expanding global infrastructure networks of transport, energy and communications to the length of all the borders between all the nation states. There are five hundred thousand kilometres of borders between nation states globally but over sixty-four million kilometres of roads, four million kilometres of railways and over one million kilometres of internet cables. His point is that we are witnessing an evolution of the world from political geography, which is how we legally divide the world, to functional geography, which is how we actually use the world.

Our global system is evolving from the vertically integrated empires of the 19th century through the horizontally interdependent nations of the 20th century into a global network civilization in the 21st century. Connectivity, not sovereignty, has become the organizing principle of the human species.

People move to cities to be connected, and connectivity is why cities thrive. They are the points of connection both internally within nation states and transnationally. Individually and collectively, the world's cities are connecting and breaking away from nation states in terms of setting the agenda for the future. The "C40 Cities" is one such progressive network of ninety-six cities from around the world, representing over seven hundred million citizens and one quarter of the global economy.

Mayors of the C40 cities are committed to delivering on the most ambitious goals of the Paris Agreement (for nations to reduce their greenhouse gas emissions). They are taking the initiative at the local level to lower these emissions as well as to clean up the air we breathe. This powerful group of cities has the resources and vision to take bold climate action. In tackling the same pervasive problems from different angles, the C40 cities work collaboratively to help each other share knowledge and accelerate the implementation of proven climate solutions.

The emergence of empowered and more self-reliant cities is not limited to the big megacities, as a dramatic example shown by U.S. cities demonstrates. When the Trump administration announced in June 2017 that the USA would withdraw from the Paris Agreement, the federal government ceded its leadership on climate change. In response, a group of more than one thousand U.S. city mayors, State governors and businesses, representing over 130 million Americans, formed the "We Are Still In" coalition vowing to uphold the agreement. They are modernity at large, representing a different, civic face of government. Municipal leaders in the USA are not throwing away their shot: they are moving in unison with a shared vision of transforming their cities entirely to renewable sources of energy. By the end of 2017, fifty cities and towns across the USA had already made this ambition of one hundred percent renewables a commitment, despite the backward federal stance.

Cascading learning and actions across an expanding number of local cities mimics nature's genius for encouraging diversity and multiplicity. Each city is a unique combination of the same universal elements, and so different solutions to common climate challenges multiply. Instead of national goals consolidated on a gigantic scale, civic goals are intensely local and diverse. The power of proliferation of different city initiatives is two-fold: when they succeed, their solutions are quickly copied and adapted; when they fail, they fail on a manageable scale with a multitude of backups in place elsewhere.

A renewed focus on cities and civic life is not simply a change in national policy – it is a fundamental change in people's perspective. The narrative is told from the point of view of our prevailing urban condition, encouraging all of us to imagine the way forward from the starting point of living together in cities. We examine the common threads that connect past revolutions with the next massive change, and the attitudes needed to make this change happen. As citizens we have no choice: the battle for a more prosperous and sustainable future will be won or lost on the streets of our cities.

Changing Direction

PAST REVOLUTIONS

To paraphrase Winston Churchill, the farther back you look the farther forward you are likely to see. Past revolutions were fundamentally revolutions in converting energy. They were upheavals in our quest for more physical energy from natural resources to power industries and meet the needs of a growing human population. They were also radical shifts in our collective imagination and beliefs that captured the renewable energy of people to shape society and direct its development in new ways. The three historical industrial revolutions and the fourth one that is underway can be characterised as a sequence of using machines to help us to do, to grow, to think and to interact.

The first industrial revolution marked the transition from doing things by using muscle power to using mechanical power, with the invention of the steam engine and mechanical production. The second, technology revolution grew that mechanical capability rapidly by making mass production possible, with the advances of electricity and assembly lines. The advent of the third, digital revolution expanded our thinking by transforming how we access knowledge and communicate, and by programming machines to "think" with more speed and dexterity than us. The current fourth industrial revolution is a progression of the digital revolution built on the fusion of pervasive mobile internet and powerful microsensors, artificial intelligence and machine learning, changing the way we interact with the world around us and, importantly, with each other.

These epochal industry shifts have been interspersed by no less important intellectual revolutions that have channelled our collective energy and reshaped social, rational and political behaviours. The cognitive revolution that occurred in our prehistory enabled humankind to cooperate effectively and flexibly in large groups, and is still the bedrock of our socio-economic behaviour and vagaries today. Much later, the first agricultural revolution domesticated our nomadic lifestyle and created a dependency on the land and on communal interaction. The scientific revolution was a transformation in our understanding of the world around us and in the power of rational thinking over superstition. More recently, the political revolution that most defines all the major political actors on the world stage today has been the creation and entrenchment of nation states.

We will look back at these global revolutions for insights that help us understand how and why we find ourselves in our current situation. Today's circumstances are not inevitable:

contemporary narratives and economic orders can undergo astonishing transformations, despite their dominance and the impression of permanence.

Less than one hundred years ago, the British Empire had a controlling influence over one-quarter of the world's population and covered almost a quarter of the Earth's total land area. For over a century, Britain had been the predominant global power, backed up by military might and the long arm of its navy. The empire was primarily an economic one driven by commerce and trade, and at its height in 1922 was the largest in history. By the late 1940s this dominant global economic order had more or less disappeared and the U.K. itself was on the brink of bankruptcy.

More recently, those who lived during the Cold War will remember how international relations were dominated for decades by two nuclear superpowers at loggerheads, the USA and USSR. Many people on both sides were confounded by the speed and suddenness of the disappearance of one superpower as the entire Soviet Union collapsed under its own weight, dissolving itself into eleven republics. Soviet President Mikhail Gorbachev resigned on 26 December 1991, declaring his office defunct, and the Soviet flag was lowered for the last time to be replaced over the Kremlin with the pre-revolutionary Russian flag.

Human civilisation is indeed fragile and its transformation from one construct to another can be very rapid despite prevailing the myths of its steadfastness. Transformation means creation as well as collapse. All around us, shifts are taking place that indicate the way we live currently is already turning into history. Some of the clues to our future trajectory lie deep in the past.

SEVENTY THOUSAND YEARS AGO

Something occurred in the evolution of hominids that enabled one particular species, Homo sapiens, to become the most dominant species on Earth. Some anthropologists refer to a cognitive revolution that enabled early humans to build up knowledge so they could change their behaviour without waiting for the change to be encoded in their DNA. This evolutionary development is what divides us from all other species and what divides our history from our biology.

Decoupled from slow genetic changes to DNA, today's descendants of early humans are able to make history by changing behaviours rapidly and cooperating socially and economically in extremely complex ways. We have learned how to shape thoughts in each other's brains through language, with spoken and written word. This ability to communicate spans time and distance as well as the barriers between strangers.

The real power of the cognitive revolution is our unique ability to talk about things that are not real. In other words, to create myths which capture lots of people's imagination and influence their behaviour in precise ways. The effects are so pervasive that we hardly recognise or distinguish some of today's myths from reality. Professor Harari elaborates on how dependent we are on our collective fictions:

Ever since the Cognitive Revolution, Sapiens have thus been living in a dual reality. On the one hand, the objective reality of rivers, trees and lions; and on the other hand, the imagined reality of gods, nations and corporations. As time went by, the imagined reality became ever more powerful so that today the very survival of rivers, trees and lions depends on the grace of imagined entities such as the United States and Google.

The cognitive revolution gave us the means to imagine an order that will destroy us and equally to imagine a future order that can sustain us. The powerful myths that shape our society and the choices we make are figments of our collective imagination; they can be reimagined when enough of us believe in a different narrative.

TWELVE THOUSAND YEARS AGO

The first agricultural revolution marked the transformation of society from a traditional hunter-gatherer lifestyle to settled farming with a reliable food supply. The transition occurred worldwide over millennia, starting in the Near East where the wild progenitors of crops such as wheat, barley and peas can be traced. There appears to be no single factor that led people to take up farming in different parts of the world. In the Near East it is believed that seasonal conditions changed at the end of the last ice age, favouring annual plants like wild cereals. In other regions, the transition may have been brought on by increased pressure on natural food resources that forced people to cultivate crops for a more secure supply.

Animal domestication occurred around the same time as plant domestication. Cattle, pigs, sheep and goats all have their origins as farmed animals in the region known as the Fertile Crescent covering eastern Turkey, Iraq and south-western Iran. Domesticated fowl were also kept around the world, with the ancestor of modern-day chickens that are found in the Americas, Europe, the Middle East and Africa originating in the Indian subcontinent. Wild horses were domesticated later, some six thousand years ago, on the grasslands of Ukraine and southwest Russia, before spreading across Europe and Asia.

Domesticating animals converted the muscle energy of animals into additional human power, used to help cultivate crops and transport goods and people, as well as for food. Dogs were the first animal species to be domesticated, and the earliest dogs appeared during the time of the hunter-gatherers. Domesticating dogs served a human need for more help with hunting and for an early warning system if danger arose, as well as for the companionship that we recognise today. Humans have been raising puppies for longer than they have been planting crops for food!

Farming and raising livestock tied people to land for cultivation and grazing, and this gave rise to permanent settlements. For tens of thousands of years the dominant social structure of human life had been small nomadic groups. After the first agricultural revolution, humans lived in fixed locations surrounded by an increasing accumulation of non-portable possessions. These settlements developed on a scale needed to run human affairs, that in turn led to job specialisation, polity, and the rise of industry and commerce.

The first agricultural revolution sowed the seeds for the growth of our cities and civilisations. Settlements were literally where people chose to organise themselves in communities tied to the land. Where we choose to settle today and how we interact with the natural world remains as fundamental to our urban future as it did to our rural past.

FOUR HUNDRED YEARS AGO

In European history the scientific revolution refers to the period between Copernicus and Newton, and was not so much a revolution in science as it was a revolution in the thought and practice that brought about modern science.

Prior to this revolution, knowledge about the natural world had traditionally been a contemplative pursuit comparable to theology. The newfound intellectual energy was converted into practical, useful knowledge based on mathematical principles and the discipline of experiments.

Polish astronomer Nicolaus Copernicus made the bold claim that the Earth moves. Not only did this claim go against common sense (people felt no physical movement) but it also contradicted the authority and orthodoxy of the church. Copernicus' insistence that the planets circle the Sun rather than Earth was a model of the heavens based on mathematics that he considered to be more coherent than believing the Earth was the stationary centre of the cosmos.

His viewpoint led more great thinkers to pursue other theories in mathematics and physics that supported this new model. There were new astronomical observations by Brahe; theoretical modifications to the orbits of planets by Kepler; and new principles of motion based on a moving Earth by Galileo, Descartes and Huygens. Isaac Newton made the final link that joined heaven and Earth by uniting celestial and terrestrial bodies under the same universal laws of motion.

According to ancient and medieval science before the scientific revolution, the world was believed to be composed of four qualities (earth, water, air and fire) and above it was ether, a material that filled the rest of the universe. By the time of Newton, the contemporary view was that the world was made of atoms or small material bodies. People no longer blindly followed the beliefs of the past. Scientific knowledge was accepted on the authority of mathematical argument and sensory evidence, not on opinion. The Royal Society was founded in London in 1660, gathering eminent scientists and physicians together, promoting scientific priority and peer review, and publishing such works as Newton's *Principia Mathematica*. "*Nullius in verba*", the motto of the Royal Society, is understood to mean "take nobody's word for it". It is an expression of the determination to withstand the domination of authority and to verify statements by appealing to facts determined by experiment.

The long-term effect of this revolution has been the modern acceptance and dependence on science and evidence as the way to think about and explain the natural world and our place within it. From the 1700s onwards, the Sun no longer orbited the Earth and man was no longer the centre of the universe. It matters that we inform our view of the future objectively, and that we view our role with commensurate humility.

TWO HUNDRED AND FIFTY YEARS AGO

The first industrial revolution began in Britain in the late eighteenth century, converting energy from muscle power into machine power by mechanising tasks done laboriously by hand. Several factors contributed to Britain's role as the birthplace of the industrial revolution. As the world's biggest colonial power at the time, Britain had unrivalled access to raw materials from its colonies for manufacturing products as well as a vast marketplace for its finished goods. At home it had significant natural deposits of coal and iron ore that were essential for industrialisation.

Before this revolution, raw materials and finished goods were hauled by horse-drawn wagons, taken by boats along canals and rivers, and sailed across oceans. All this changed after the first viable steam engine was introduced in 1712. By the middle of the nineteenth century, steam engines dominated land and sea transport, and were essential to power every decent-sized manufacturing factory in the industrialised world.

The second industrial revolution, also known as the technological revolution, began in the late nineteenth century with the advent of electricity converting mechanical power into electrical power. It was a time of great imagination and full of inventions. Large-scale power stations enabled the operation of assembly lines for mass production. Manufacturing was reshaped so profoundly that bigger companies that did not adopt assembly lines simply went out of business. The introduction of public electricity led to inventions such as the light bulb, telephone and electric streetcars. Stronger and cheaper steel replaced iron, making it possible to build more railway tracks and to build bigger ships, skyscrapers and bridges. The internal combustion engine was invented, powering a new mass-produced automobile industry.

Despite the historical perspective, the second industrial revolution has yet to be fully experienced by seventeen percent of the world, with 1.3 billion people lacking access to electricity. The demand for electricity globally will continue to grow as underserved populations catch up, personal incomes rise and power-hungry cities expand. It is not a trend that is going to reverse in our lifetime. How we meet this future demand determines our future.

TWO HUNDRED YEARS AGO
A huge amount of political energy has been expended globally in creating nation states, replacing former empires, kingdoms and city-states. The establishment of territories as sovereign

states that are central to world order and international law is a relatively new phenomenon. When the United States became a nation state in 1788, there were around twenty nation states; by 1945, half of all the modern states that exist today were in place; today there are over 190 sovereign states around the world.

Professors Wimmer and Feinstein at the University of California studied 145 of today's states from 1816 to the year that each became a state. They tested three established theories as to why nation states have proliferated across the globe: modernisation, world polity and historical institutionalism. The first theory explains the rise of nation states based on the effects of industrialisation and the modernising impact of the industrial revolutions around the world. According to this theory, the increasing complexities of production, trade and commerce spurred domestic political changes that resulted in the formation of states. The second theory of world polity examines how the concepts of sovereignty, progress and human rights acquired great authority and provided a common framework for the actions of individuals across the globe. Nation states and transnational institutions were shaped from the crystallisation of this rational world order.

The third theory of historical institutionalism bases the creation of nation states on the legacy of institutional structures. For example, the success or failure of a national revolution to overthrow the elite would depend heavily on the structure of the country's institutions in the pre-revolutionary period and how much these pre-existing legal, financial and governing institutions went on to support the outcome of the revolution. The conclusion of their research is surprising:

We find no evidence for the effects of industrialization, the advent of mass literacy, or increasingly direct rule, which are associated with the modernization theories... Nor is the growing global hegemony of the nation state model a good predictor of individual instances of nation state formation... We conclude that the global rise of the nation state is driven by proximate and contextual political factors situated at the local and regional levels, in line with historical institutionalist arguments.

In other words, successful nation states have been created not out of industrial necessity, increasing complexities of the modern world or the influence of a common culture, but from the will of the people locally and the support of their civic institutions. The conclusion is powerful because it recognises citizens and their self-governance structures as the agents of transformative change.

Although almost all of us were born into one, the concept of a nation state is still new and imperfect. Nation states vary significantly in practice based on the values and beliefs of the people locally and if they are ruled by a sovereign, strong-armed by a dictator, or governed by elected representatives. Nationality is supposed to bind the citizen to the state but we may not necessarily choose our nation state as the place that best defines us. A stronger place of identity may be called for that is much closer to home.

FIFTY YEARS AGO

The digital revolution began in the 1960s and marks the beginning of the current information era. The development of semiconductors and microprocessors enabled the transfer of energy from mechanical technology to digital electronics. The early mainframe computers that resulted were enormous room-sized metal boxes or frames, requiring large amounts of electrical power and air-conditioning. They would frequently burn out or short-circuit when bugs flew into the system. Getting a computer bug refers back to a time when moths were a problem in early mainframes!

The microchip led to computers becoming smaller and the advent of personal computers. As late as 1977, Ken Olsen, founder of Digital Equipment Corporation (a major company in the development of computing), made the infamous quip, "There is no reason anyone would want a computer in their home." His prediction proved to be woefully wrong. A proposal for the World Wide Web, originally called "The Mesh", was written by Tim Berners-Lee in 1989 to persuade researchers at CERN, a particle-physics laboratory near Geneva, to use a global hypertext system for information sharing.

It turned out that CERN was not the only interested user in The Mesh. The web became commercialised in 1995 with the first sales on Amazon.com and Echo Bay (which later became eBay). A year later, HoTMaiL (the capitalised letters were a homage to HTML) became the world's first free web-based email service. Google launched in 1998, revolutionising the way people find information online; Wikipedia followed in 2001, paving the way for collective web content generation. The term "social media" was coined in 2004 as sites and web applications allowed users to create and share their own content. Notable newcomers were Thefacebook (2004), YouTube (2005), Twitter (2006) and iPhone (2007), which was almost entirely responsible for the take-off of the mobile web.

The ubiquity of internet access is the crowning point of the digital revolution to date. Where this has occurred it has transformed, for better or for worse, the way people find and share information. Individuals have almost limitless knowledge at their fingertips at the same time as their daily lives have become saturated with social media, fake news and online shopping. Organisations are more efficient, can extend their reach and make better decisions, yet have become more vulnerable to cyber attacks, online fraud and security breaches. We have a Faustian pact with the likes of Facebook and Google, sacrificing personal content and intimate details in order to satisfy our desire for online connections. Faceless algorithms filter information by profiling individuals so each person sees only a mirrored view of the world. It is easier to reach people but harder to get their attention.

The digital revolution has given us an essential network for building a knowledge-based economy but it has also left us with two challenges: a dilemma and a divide. Those societies that have undergone the digital transformation face the dilemma of how to reap the social and economic benefits while mitigating the harmful consequences. As the digital benefits have grown, so too have the disadvantages of missing out – increasing the fear that the divide between the digital "haves" and "have-nots" grows ever wider. Almost half of the world's population have not: nearly four billion people are without internet access.

Despite the divide, digital connectivity will undoubtedly continue to pull people together virtually and physically. Local is no longer parochial but is networked as voices and actions are amplified across borders. Acting locally in a connected world will have more impact than ever before.

TODAY

We are on the brink of the fourth industrial revolution in some parts of the world, a disruption caused by the pervasive power of digitisation and information technology. The shift in how we can use machines to interact with the world is all around us, from implantable technologies to autonomous vehicles to artificial intelligence.

Consider the example of 3D printing, also known as additive manufacturing. A product is designed on a computer and made using a 3D printer that creates a solid object by building successive layers of material. The printer can work unattended to make both simple and complicated objects, from hearing aids to blades for wind turbines. In time, 3D printers could be used at home to make a wide array of everyday objects affordably, democratising the power of product creation and manufacture, and reducing the need for long supply chains.

Researchers are already working on 4D printing (the extra dimension stands for "dynamic") where materials are layered at a cellular or geometric level in such a way that the object activates, assembles or repairs itself in response to changes in atmospheric temperature or pressure. By design, the 4D object converts the ambient energy from its surroundings in order to do the work for you. Metal alloys with shape memory recover their initial shape when deformed; self-sensing biomedical implants attach themselves; underwater devices activate independently at certain depths. As Skylar Tibbits, research director of MIT's Self-Assembly Lab, comments:

What we're really trying to make is robots without robots. We want to design materials that can transform themselves when exposed to energy, but which don't necessarily require circuit boards, electronics, or other moving parts to operate.

No less radical in the transfer of energy from people into objects is the expanding network of internet-enabled microelectronics and actuators embedded into physical devices and vehicles, to enable them to exchange data and work independently. According to a report from BI Intelligence, there will be a staggering twenty-three billion devices connected to the internet by 2021. This web of interactive objects known as the "internet of things" has the power to impact virtually every aspect of daily life and reshape how industries operate, from agriculture to healthcare to transportation.

For example, cars are increasingly becoming computers on wheels in the shift towards self-driving vehicles. Most new cars manufactured today are internet-enabled, connected to cloud-based traffic and navigation services, able to receive real-time traffic alerts and emergency roadside assistance. The big automotive manufacturers are currently vying with internet giants such as Baidu and Google, and contenders such as Tesla and Uber, to lead the transformation from vehicles driven by humans to vehicles that drive themselves.

Klaus Schwab is founder and executive chairman of the World Economic Forum. In his book *The Fourth Industrial Revolution* he outlines twenty-one technology shifts that are already underway as a result of this fusion of technologies and their connectivity. These are profound and systemic changes across physical, digital and biological domains – smart cities, self-learning machines, neurotechnologies – with tipping points when these changes become mainstream estimated in years not decades. Schwab's conviction is that this revolution will be every bit as powerful, impactful and historically important as the previous three industrial revolutions. Despite his enthusiasm for these breakthroughs, he acknowledges his concern that as we stand on the brink we are missing a collective vision of where we are heading:

The world lacks a consistent, positive and common narrative that outlines the opportunities and challenges of the fourth industrial revolution, a narrative that is essential if we are to empower a diverse set of individuals and communities.

The pace of change and speed of travel is faster than ever before, and yet if we do not know where we are going we will never get there. Another industrial revolution in itself is not the answer.

THE YEARS AHEAD

Planetary boundaries are environmental red lines that we cannot safely cross without putting life at risk. We have already exceeded four of these limits, calling nature's bluff that a cascade of harmful effects will be triggered. Ecosystems are changing in response to our transgressions, as some collapse alarmingly while others slump almost imperceptibly towards irreversible tipping points. The future looks perilous if we continue to damage the environment irreparably for our own myopic ends.

Throughout our history we have been converting energy from one form to another so that more people can do more. We live by the stories we are told, and reshape the world by the new stories we tell. The starting point of early human society is characterised by its localisation, using resources sustainably, sharing a common purpose and living in harmony with nature. The long arc of history bends our society towards its origin – towards increasing decentralisation, the need for carbon-free energy, shared imperatives and living within our means. From five million people ten thousand years ago to almost eight billion today, this starting point will look very different when we return.

CIVIC REVOLUTION

Our whole way of living is already passing into history. We are past the final "no" of denial that we can keep on doing what we're doing. To quote from a poem by Wallace Stevens, the American Modernist, "After the final no there comes a yes, and on that yes the future world depends." So where does this leave you, if we really are on the brink of massive change? One action is to jump into the political fray, if that is your calling. For the rest of us, the other action is to jump into civic life and what we can do as citizens.

Revolutions are fundamental changes in power and organisations in response to the urgent demands and actions of the population. They are ignited by discontent with the status quo and fuelled by a narrative of hope and vision of a better future. The migration of people from rural areas into towns and cities has set the stage but is not in itself the revolution. The point of inflection is not that the majority of the people around the world now live in urban areas, but how differently this increasing population of city dwellers chooses to live. The fundamental change in urban living will be hastened by the need to prevent catastrophic ecological harm; the vision of solutions that are not extraordinary and within our grasp; and the hope that we can continue to prosper by changing what we do.

The next revolution is neither agricultural nor industrial, but civic. It is about transforming places. At the same time it is an intellectual revolution about our civic state of mind. The aspiration of the civic revolution is lasting social and economic vitality locally, for civilisation as a whole. It is not hope that leads to action so much as action that leads to hope. You get to tell your own story of hope if you take action.

This civic transformation will be a collective response to imperatives that we cannot ignore and will be the result of dramatic shifts in personal attitudes towards our current predicament. As evidence continues to build of climate change and mass extinction, and scientific warnings grow louder, a rapidly growing number of people already believe we are facing a crisis that requires immediate action.

The trigger for you may be a very real emergency such as too little water when your metropolitan area runs dry or too much water when hit by widespread flooding or violent storms; it may be the pollution you breathe in or the pollution you see outside; or it may be a symbolic indicator that sinks your heart, perhaps when an endangered species dies or when a river becomes biologically dead.

The Intergovernmental Panel on Climate Change provides evidence and expertise to people who lead at all levels in society, to inform them how best to take action. In their recent 2014 assessment they emphasise that the next two decades present a window of opportunity for mitigation in urban areas. A large portion of the world's urban areas will be developed during this period and the built environment has not yet been "locked in". They stress the need for mutually reinforcing urban policies and citizen-led initiatives to reduce our impact, from co-locating high residential with high employment densities to embracing energy efficiency; from higher diversity and integration of land uses to shunning private motorised vehicles in favour of public transport.

Unfortunately there is no silver bullet. Cities can be characterised in many different ways, from the size of population and economy to the quality of governance and social cohesion. They vary from dense, affluent cities typified by national capitals to sprawling lower-income cities growing rapidly in developing regions or declining where regional economies have stalled; from powerful megacities with more clout than nation states to nimble innovator cities that model futuristic urban living.

In simplifying such an eclectic mix, it is unhelpful to consider some as developed or advanced and others as underdeveloped or laggards: all cities are developing. No one city has the solution, as each is unique to its place and context, and every city must adapt continuously as it grows up or grows old. Neither is a single economic metric such as average income or Gross Metro Product constructive, as it simply perpetuates an economic rat race as the supposed proxy for achieving urban vitality.

Instead, cities of all types can be characterised as having either a legacy or a leapfrog perspective. Legacy cities have well-established urban infrastructure and civic services, with significant capital invested over many years. These cities may enjoy the advantage of a well-built urban environment that lends itself to increased comforts and convenience, as well as face the challenge of being locked into obsolete systems that are difficult or expensive to replace. Leapfrog cities are not invested to the same extent in the level or quality of their infrastructure or in particular technologies, and their residents may be underserved by comparison. However, they do not need to tread the same path as legacy cities in their development by sinking capital into obsolete infrastructure, or by polluting first and then spending even more to clean up afterwards. They are not locked in and can jump to alternative systems that befit the reindustrialisation of our time.

There are many exciting new technologies that will catalyse change and more are emerging all the time. However, we will not be spending our time on Elon Musk's adventures, the prowess of Google's data-driven Smart Cities, or the dreams of intercity Hyperloop travel. The story of our time is not one of technology disruption but of behaviour disruption. The civic revolution is not rocket science; it is more complicated. The attitude towards solutions based on technology innovation is too often one of "if you build it, they will come". We spend disproportionate time and resources developing and testing the science and neglect the crucial last mile of how to change human behaviour, so that people make better choices.

Invariably we do not act as rationally as economists or technologists always assume. Billions of dollars are spent on fuel-efficient technologies, for example, and yet how much is invested in a similarly exacting and systematic way into changing human behaviours so we use energy more efficiently? This last human step is too often the stumbling block in urban development if citizens do not see why they should change, and progress invariably hindered if we do not take the lead.

In an alternative view of how future events could unfold on a global scale, Paul Gilding and Jorgen Randers presented a research paper in 2010 based on the idea of a "global crisis plan" that would be needed when public opinion escalates to such an extent that global society finally decides additional policy action is needed at the supranational level. While it is unlikely that a global plan is the solution, it is undisputed that "society is capable of responding dramatically to major threats when there is acceptance of a crisis. At that point, all previous arguments against action are consigned to the dustbin."

According to their research, it is both economically feasible and possible with existing technology to rapidly reduce greenhouse gas concentrations to a level that will bring global warming back below one degree Celsius. Their plan starts forcefully with phase one modelled on a level of mobilisation over five years only previously seen during a world war. The second phase of climate neutrality is a fifteen-year-long push to lock in the achievements of the emergency reductions in greenhouse gases, and to move the world to net zero climate emissions by the end of that period.

The final climate recovery phase is the long-haul effort over a period of eighty years to create both a stable climate and a sustainable global economy. This recovery requires a long period of negative emissions to move the climate back towards pre-industrial levels of greenhouse gas concentrations. Leadership by nation states and coordination between them will be crucial, for instance by imposing a harmonised carbon tax and ceasing all pollution subsidies.

An important insight from their work is that many of the steps outlined can already be taken independently by cities, without the prerequisite of a new multinational command structure or diktat of a global plan. What would be some of the policies and actions in such a crisis plan? The initial "climate war" (their wording, not mine) phase includes closing one thousand dirty coal power plants; launching an urgent efficiency campaign matched with power rationing; building a wind turbine or solar plant in every town of one thousand inhabitants and over; rationing the use of dirty vehicles by fifty percent; reducing air travel by ten percent each year; moving society away from a diet of climate-unfriendly protein; and reducing deforestation and other logging by fifty percent.

For every programme that curtails current negative practices there would be a corresponding step along a more positive path. For example, by delivering immediate power savings with mass retrofit programmes; switching to hybrid vehicles; shifting to electronic communication and away from air travel; producing protein with lower emissions; funding regions for the climate services provided by their intact forests.

The people-led *"gilets jaunes"* protests in France at the end of 2018 demonstrate the importance of progressive implementation of government-led policies. Progressive in terms of fairness, not slowness. What started as a demonstration in Paris about an environmental tax was inflamed by a sense of financial injustice of reforms that hit hardest those with least disposable income. It is clear that such policies go up in smoke when people are penalised for doing something they feel they cannot avoid. France may have a strong tradition of civil unrest, but this impulse for a fairer social contract in transforming the status quo goes way beyond the political left or the city of Paris.

It is hard to imagine people making radical changes without resistance, or how quickly existing opposition could disappear. However, Gilding and Randers assert:

While all these actions may seem draconian or unrealistic by the standards of today's debate, they will seem far less so when society moves to a war footing and a focus on "what is necessary".

People will argue rightly that our plight is not a war in the conventional sense, of fighting one another or of a sudden threat to life that demands immediate action. However, peace does not mean an absence of conflicts. We are called to fend off a clear and present existential threat to our collective livelihood. It is tempting to ignore this or appease the incumbents, to wait and see what happens, hoping that things will get better of their own accord or that a global crisis plan will materialise in time to lead sweeping changes. As individuals this is not a plan we can control or take action on, and current populist movements make this global ambition a very distant vision. The version of events where we continue as before for as long as possible is at best wishful thinking and is increasingly discredited as wilfully blind.

Civic revolution demands a different perspective, not a political leaning. Instead of left to right, the spectrum is turned on its head from horizontal to vertical; from political parties of different colours to citizens, communities and cities of all colours. Viewed from this angle, the beliefs are more encompassing and representative of a new stage. They are self-evident yet transformative: energy is the fundamental resource that shapes our economy; growth is no longer the supreme good; the goal is lasting social and economic vitality; we face the same imperatives everywhere; nothing will change if we do not change.

These beliefs are perhaps the universal design principles for how cities should be built to last, and how we should embrace the place where we live in order to prosper. A mark of your personal readiness is how intuitive they feel to you. For many they are simply common sense, and therein lies the hope that this new civicism is not a leap of faith but rather a new outlook on what we already value, and a renewed appreciation of what we undervalue.

ENERGY IS THE FUNDAMENTAL RESOURCE.

Energy is a more fundamental resource than money in driving the economy. Our society and how it evolves is powered by the energy of people. The built environment around us, trade and industry, transportation and more, are powered by the energy of natural resources. As demand continues to rise we find ourselves at an energy crossroads as we struggle to see a way to meet the increasing needs of the world's population and the growing wants of a global economy. The path we have been following leads straight uphill and it is clear that we are going to run out of energy if we keep climbing. The signpost reads "business as usual" and points towards burning more fossil fuels and the expansive consumption of energy and materials. The other path is flat but winding. We have enough energy to keep going but there are more twists and turns along the way. This signpost reads "diversion" and points towards renewable energy, increasing current usage rather than future consumption, and collective action taken locally. The familiar path is increasingly treacherous; the alternative path is new.

To step away from the familiar with confidence, we need a bigger vision for a sustainable future than making the impact of humankind smaller. The world's population is almost eight billion and may yet reach ten billion people by the end of this century. We need a collective vision of how to prosper as we regenerate an environment that must support all of us. At its core, the man-made ecological crisis is not climate change or loss of biodiversity. It is overshoot. As we shall explore further, the diversion leads us to a state of equilibrium, and in addressing the cause of overshoot provides relief from the dire ecological symptoms that otherwise we will not be able to avoid.

The common currency of energy circulates in different ways but always starts at the level of individuals. Individual energy is converted into social capital – the bonds between people with a shared sense of place and identity – through interactions with one another and the contributions individuals make, firstly within their communities and then more broadly to society. The foundation for cooperation, exchange and innovation is based on these links and the values we share that enable us to trust each other and work together.

Civic energy channels this individual energy by shifting the perspective from person to place, from striving against each other to overcome individual problems to striving together to overcome shared problems. Some of the most pressing challenges we are facing are too big for us individually, yet cannot be solved by the state or market forces alone. The solution is not to ignore the levers of state or the markets, but to build on their strengths. The answer is to restore systems that are not so big that they cannot respond to us, but not so small that they cannot tackle the scale of the changes. Powered by civic energy, these systems are built around the places where people live, and are anchored in local communities and parts of the economy. In this way civic energy is converted into common causes that engage local citizens, such as the collaboration needed to face the imperatives of our time.

Collective energy is the broadest and most inclusive level, encompassing not only civic power but also the essential contributions of other stakeholders such as regional and national government and corporations. Outcomes range from the wealth of local community assets and employment opportunities to the regeneration of common resources such as fresh water and clean air. Collective energy is converted into a prosperous and sustainable form of urbanism.

GROWTH IS NO LONGER THE SUPREME GOOD.
Earth Overshoot Day is the calculated calendar date when humanity's resource consumption for the year exceeds Earth's capacity to regenerate those resources that year. For the rest of the year we are overdrawn: we are living on resources stolen from future generations, depleting the stock of natural capital and accumulating more carbon dioxide in the atmosphere. Each year we are falling into debt sooner. In 2000, Earth Overshoot Day fell in late September. In 2018, we started to steal from our children on the first day of August.

Previous industrial revolutions were growth oriented, converting energy to help humankind do more or produce more, or to think faster and interact smarter so that we could do even more or produce even more. In contrast, the civic revolution is growth agnostic and its aim is not to grow cities or for cities to increase their demand for more resources. As long ago as 1848, John Stuart Mill wrote in his *Principles of Political Economy*:

If the earth must lose that great portion of its pleasantness which it owes to things that the unlimited increase of wealth and population would extirpate from it, for the mere purpose of enabling it to support a larger, but not a better or a happier population, I sincerely hope, for the sake of posterity, that they will be content to be stationary, long before necessity compels them to it.

Given the dogma of endless economic growth, this shift to address overshoot is so profound that it is considered to be a heresy. And yet job creation and economic wellbeing can be realised by taking a different, regenerative route. We shall examine some of the ways that exist to increase prosperity without growth and to grow without material consumption. Clean growth may be achieved as cities grow, and equally as cities that are not growing switch to more low-carbon energy supplies. Circular economies create new opportunities for employment and internal growth through the very process of decreasing our dependency on external resources and by reducing waste.

The uneven pattern of urban migration will lead to significant growth in some cities but not others. The United Nations predicts that the number of megacities with populations of over ten million people will increase from thirty-one in 2017 to forty-one by 2030. (For perspective, forty years ago there were only three urban centres around the world – Tokyo, New York and Mexico City – that had eight-figure populations.) More than ninety percent of the future population growth to 2050 will be accounted for by the larger cities in Asia and Africa, although rapid growth is not necessarily these cities' goal. Urbanisation that fails to bring about inclusive growth results in more urban poverty, the proliferation of informal settlements and rising inequality. In these regions cities are not seeking growth as the means to increase prosperity but instead are seeking to maintain prosperity in spite of their growth.

THE GOAL IS LASTING SOCIAL AND ECONOMIC VITALITY. The rising social and economic influence of cities within nations and internationally has a profound effect on the balance of political and commercial power around the world. Ironically the trend towards subsidiarity and acting locally is growing across the globe with the result that more local power is being exercised in more places. The connectivity between these places ensures that the influence of their power is more fluid than fragmented. The same dynamic is taking place in towns within regions, as these urban hubs are yet another source of concentrated energy. Across the different urban scales individual energy spills into local civic energy into momentum behind more widespread collective energy.

We are reminded of the adage that several additional Earths would be needed if all of us were to spend our energy living in a suburban house with two cars, flying on holidays and with work, enjoying a diet heavy in meat, and more. Although this constraint seems obvious, it does not necessarily follow that rising standards of living cannot be reconciled with finite resources. The Earth's carrying capacity – the number of people that the environment can sustain indefinitely – is not a fixed number, and varies from as little as two billion people living a middle-class American lifestyle to forty billion people if humans still lived as hunter-gatherers consuming only what they needed.

The way we live in cities and how cities operate around us are the key to restoring the balance with our habitat without regressing to pre-technology tribalism. The ecological genius of the city enables us to live better on less instead of living better on more. There are unrealised environmental efficiencies and societal benefits inherent in the high densities of urban settlements. The goal of lasting social and economic vitality locally, for civilisation as a whole, is within our grasp if we address the big imperatives.

WE FACE THE SAME IMPERATIVES EVERYWHERE.
There will always be pressure on cities from citizens to do a better job in maintaining safety and security, building housing, improving education, creating employment opportunities,

delivering quality healthcare and social services. All these things are necessary, some are urgent, and none are sufficient in a resource-constrained world with an unstable environment.

Although there are considerable differences between us in the essentials we would like to fix or improve in our city, we need bigger aspirations that alleviate these pressures at the same time as they enable us to move in the direction of lasting prosperity. We must be more deliberate in where our energy is generated and in how it is expended, because this will drive the new economy; be passionate in how we look after vital ecosystems, so that they can support us indefinitely; be wise in what constitutes wealthy living, in order that we might reach our goal.

All of us face the same three imperatives in addressing an unsustainable economy and an unstable environment. Firstly, we need an economy that is restorative, an inversion from making people more productive to making natural resource systems more productive. Secondly, we are compelled, existentially and morally, to protect biodiversity as it supports and sustains our entire way of life. And thirdly, we must strive for more social equity as the key to making the transformation by unlocking the potential energy of people.

These three imperatives are connected: we cannot protect biodiversity without a restorative economy; we cannot build such an economy without grassroots participation; and we cannot hold communities together or keep economies from collapsing if ecosystem services are failing. When we address any one of these imperatives directly, our effort has the power to transform. The collective result is structural change to the imbalances in our way of life and in our interaction with the environment. The outcome is a change in the narrative.

NOTHING WILL CHANGE IF WE DO NOT CHANGE.
We are not above nature, despite living in the Anthropocene era. It only takes one "extreme weather" event for this hard truth to sink home. This message was repeated throughout 2018. The east coast of America suffered some of its lowest temperatures on record during the winter while California had the deadliest wildfire in its history in November. Snow fell in the Sahara desert where average temperatures are usually around thirty-seven degrees Celsius. Japan witnessed its highest-ever temperatures, followed by some of the worst flooding and landslides in a generation. Heavy rain and flooding affected large parts of China, with over two hundred rivers flooding their banks in Sichuan and Henan. The devastation in the state of Kerala in India caused by the annual monsoon rains was the worst in nearly one hundred years, with more than fifty thousand people displaced. More devastation happened elsewhere and sadly more will follow.

For a human culture that rests on the need for control, bending to the will of nature feels unnatural. It is a big shift in perspective to be willing to change our attitudes and habits to accommodate very real natural boundaries instead of attempting to extend them to meet new desires. Overshoot is not a supply problem for technology to solve. The problem lies on the demand side and in our depredation. It occurs in cities that face the challenges of modernising locked-in infrastructure, and in cities young enough or lacking in a built legacy to leap forward by taking a very different development path. Solutions for both places are desperately needed if we are to achieve change with greater scale and speed.

The rest of the citizen's guide focuses on answers to the question, "What happens when we change our minds?" What is the upshot when we are empowered and take more control of our civic life; become inventive and work with nature; include more people in making our city a home? Shifts in our civic attitudes are brought to life by some of the possible outcomes illustrated. Time is not on our side. The enemy of this "war" on climate change – if our war is thought of as a common cause that demands mass mobilisation – is procrastination. Thousands of species are being killed on our watch and they will never return. Whatever you think you can do, don't delay.

Using Power

CLIMATE CHANGE

What should we do if the risks of climate chaos are too grave to ignore? The answer is drastic. We rebuild the foundation of our economy so that it is restorative and not injurious. Energy is the fundamental resource that shapes the economy, so we must start by weaning ourselves off oil and gas as the basis, and pursue "clean growth" as the alternative. Clean growth requires not only the replacement of fossil fuels by renewables but also profound changes in our energy consumption. It involves nothing less than the reindustrialisation of our society, and citizens must take the lead rather than today's industry incumbents.

Consider one of the more recent transformative industries – the internet – and how much it has changed the way we work and socialise; how it has empowered individuals and organisations alike; how it has influenced the flow of ideas and things around the world. During the internet boom the capital needed was low (Google, for example, needed a mere twenty-five million dollars), the market potential could be measured in billions, and what was at stake was finding old friends and buying new stuff. In contrast, the transformation to a restorative economy requires capital investments in clean-tech across many different sectors, the market potential is measured in trillions in whichever currency you choose and the stakes are much higher.

The availability of capital should not be the determining factor in achieving clean growth. The radical innovation needed to overhaul legacy cities is also an opportunity for citizens in leapfrog cities to take a different pathway, bypassing the high capital investments of the past. The development of telephony before the arrival of the internet is a textbook case: "POTS" (Plain Old Telephone Services) required massive capital investments to connect millions of landlines with copper wire, until the advent of low-capital mobile cellular made much of the POTS infrastructure redundant. Today the number of mobile phone users worldwide is almost five billion and cellular communication is an unprecedented technological revolution. The impact has been most profound in Africa, with its landline coverage of less than two fixed-line subscriptions per one hundred people but almost sixty-five mobile subscriptions. Instead of playing catch-up, people in countries with underdeveloped POTS simply overtook the landline technology on which the legacy countries were still dependent.

Today, over one billion people are currently without electricity, predominantly in Asia and Africa. India is a case in point: the country is chronically short of power and Indian cities experience temporary power cuts all too often. With their growing urban populations and increasing standard of living, these cities will require even more energy in the future. Like the leapfrog in telephony, serving residents in areas with insufficient grid electricity today will be fundamentally different from the past. Increasingly, citizens in underserved neighbourhoods can choose more affordable, renewable energy alternatives without waiting for the grid. They shape a trajectory for expansion that diverges from legacy cities, a leapfrog path that does not first pollute with conventional fuels and then incur more cost afterwards to clean up.

Unfortunately national trading programmes for pollutants such as greenhouse gases are distracting market-based schemes that do not deal directly with the industry challenge. The European Union's carbon trading scheme is currently the largest in the world, until China implements the plans it announced in early 2018 to move to a national carbon market. In these and other carbon trading schemes, polluters that qualify hold allowances equal in amount to their emissions, and those who want to increase their emissions buy permits from others willing to sell. Based on economic theory the polluters who can reduce emissions most cheaply will do so, achieving overall emission reductions at the lowest cost to society. Having created a market for permits, financial derivatives of carbon credits can then happily be traded and speculated on secondary markets.

Selling carbon credits is reminiscent of the medieval practice of selling indulgences. There was no evidence that these remissions worked, but there was plenty of money to be made helping everyone feel better. At best, emissions trading schemes are a transitory policy tool to send a market signal to companies and investors to shift away from heavily polluting sources. At worst, they are complicated financial mechanisms that add delays and provide very little financial imperative for polluters to switch to clean energy. The focus should be on treating greenhouse gases as dangerous pollutants rather than tradable derivatives; we should spend our energies on reducing emissions whatever the source, instead of devising trading rules for a shell game.

In practice, carbon pricing and speculation makes policy enforcement more difficult not less. The beleaguered EU Emissions Trading Scheme had a surplus of more than two billion permits in 2014, with each allowance giving the polluter the right to emit one ton of carbon dioxide. When the number of permits outstrips demand (which can clearly happen from European Union experience) market forces only serve to make them cheaper and further decrease the economic incentive to change. China's emissions trading scheme will be much bigger in size than the European Union scheme, although it will still account for only a fraction of the country's total emissions. There won't be a fixed cap on the carbon emissions covered by the new scheme, so the total volume of pollutants can continue to rise even if power producers become more efficient.

Fortunately China's trading scheme has been developed in the context of a much wider range of national climate policies that will have greater influence on reducing carbon emissions in the near term. There are a lot of positive changes within China's energy sector and on climate policies that are exciting; its emissions trading scheme is not one of them.

BP's *Energy Outlook* report on the global energy market appears much the same each year: oil and gas demand will continue to grow; global energy use will continue to rise; renewables are growing fast, but from such a small base that they do not change the bigger picture. As if BP were living on a different planet, the company dispassionately forecasts that the carbon emissions in their "evolving transition" scenario will miss the target reductions of the Paris Agreement that are there to avoid climate catastrophe. Given the oil giant's vested interests, it is an outlook you would expect to reaffirm the solidity of BP's core non-renewable business without dwelling too much on the inconvenience of global warming. Somewhat disingenuously, BP's Chief Executive Officer Bob Dudley observes that we need "a far more decisive break from the past" while calling for effective carbon pricing to ensure that market signals will change our behaviour as needed.

Hope from this *Energy Outlook* is found in between the annual updates, in how the projections for our mix of energy are revised from one year to the next. BP has repeatedly underestimated the growth of renewables at the same time as it has overestimated the demand for coal. In fact, BP has had to raise its projections for wind and solar energy every year – for the last seven years. Change is in the air. There is a similar story to be told in its underforecasting of electric vehicles, as people's willingness to change continues to exceed industry expectations.

BP and the rest of Big Oil are too vested financially in a far more dangerous, slower-paced transition to be in the vanguard of redesigning the energy and mobility sectors. Like tobacco companies before them, they are increasingly out of step with the groundswell of demand from citizens to reduce the harm they cause to our health by damage they inflict on the environment, or to take more care of the air that we breathe.

The most important observation we can make is that even the largest oil and gas incumbents cannot refute the accelerating growth in renewables on a global scale as citizens and companies switch to cleaner alternatives. A more realistic outlook would likely still be too low, as the unspoken task is for BP to predict the tipping point of an energy revolution that turns on the tide of public opinion, not the choreography of industry insiders. For those bold enough to call it, the comment by Arthur C. Clarke goes further:

If we have learned one thing from the history of invention and discovery, it is that in the long run – and often in the short one – the most daring prophecies seem laughably conservative.

Switching to renewable energy supplies is a big step forward in cutting global greenhouse gas emissions by eighty to ninety percent, as the Intergovernmental Panel on Climate Change says is needed. The second step involves reducing our overall demand for energy, by radically improving energy efficiency and by recirculating resources and materials. Cities are the places where we should focus our efforts, as they are inevitably aggregators of raw materials, components and goods. According to the Ellen MacArthur Foundation, cities account not only for sixty to eighty percent of all greenhouse gas emissions but also for seventy-five percent of natural resource consumption and fifty percent of global waste production.

The incredible power behind the idea of circular economies is that it would effectively separate economic growth from resource usage by reducing our dependency on primary materials and energy. We already know that our linear "take, make, consume, dispose" way of life is unsustainable. In a circular economy, we would not necessarily need to consume more stuff for the economy to grow, and conversely we could stop consuming stuff without fear of the economy collapsing. Increasing the frantic consumption of disposable products would no longer be the goal. The revolution in how we use resources more efficiently to create "circular cities" is no less fundamental than the empowerment of cities that are self-sufficient in renewable energy.

Industries and cities redesign the way they work on circular principles by reducing materials, waste and pollution during the upfront stage of product development or infrastructure design; by finding innovative ways of extending the useful life of components and materials; by offering services instead of selling products. Citizens do so more intuitively by relentlessly refusing, reducing, reusing and recycling.

As the Ellen MacArthur Foundation outlines, the quest to remake cities as circular cities would support existing urban policies by encouraging an innovative urban economy with a wider distributed manufacturing base and new forums for sharing and exchange. It would boost local employment by creating new work opportunities such as repair and recycling services. Reduced consumption of primary materials and lower material usage would automatically decrease carbon emissions as well as the spending on procurement and waste management. To put more succinctly:

A circular city seeks to generate prosperity, increase liveability, and improve resilience for the city and its citizens, while aiming to decouple the creation of value from the consumption of finite resources.

In striving to create a restorative economy, renewable energy and circularity are two sides of the same coin. We cannot achieve clean growth if the economy depends on burning more fossil fuels, or if growth depends on consuming more primary materials. It is time for citizens to lead by example, taking back control and being infinitely more resourceful.

EMPOWERMENT

The climate problem is mostly an energy problem. The energy industry as a whole is in the spotlight as its greenhouse gas emissions are responsible for about two-thirds of the grave we are digging for ourselves. Reducing the carbon intensity of electricity generation is vital, as decarbonising this industry can happen more rapidly than in manufacturing, building or transport. As citizens we play one of the leading roles in this transition, not only as energy consumers but also as future producers.

The rules of the game have changed in many countries as the supply of energy has been transformed by two very significant developments. First came liberalisation and the unbundling of vertically integrated utilities, introducing competition in power generation and energy retailing. Second came financial incentives for renewable energy that were literally a breath of fresh air in the surrounding fug of fossil fuel subsidies.

According to the International Energy Agency, the estimated total value of all the fossil fuel consumption subsidies around the world was a breath-stopping 300 billion dollars in 2017. As a point of comparison, the G20 nations provide four times more public financing to fossil fuels than to renewable energy. Such gargantuan sums of money hinder progress towards a cleaner and more efficient energy future by distorting fossil fuel's real market value and discounting its true environmental cost. Two very valid objections, and why the International Energy Agency continues to advocate efforts to get them removed.

Wind, water and solar power all make money, but given their localised nature they will never supply the concentrated profits that multinational oil and gas companies expect from the likes of a single oil field. Conversely, for municipalities that have not enjoyed the windfall of generating local energy for their residents, the decentralisation of energy supplies is their gain.

Decentralisation of renewables is an unstoppable force for several good reasons: local energy generation improves security of supply; it is more environmentally friendly; and increasingly it is cost-effective despite the persistent bias towards subsidising fossil fuels. And yet the pending disruption is not simply a tussle for control taking place over our heads between fossil fuel giants and energy newcomers. Instead, a more fundamental shift in attitude and decision-making is happening, from hierarchical central planning and command-and-control to local empowerment and a sense of ownership in how our energy is generated.

Christoph Burger and Jens Weinmann, senior lecturers and researchers at the European School of Management and Technology, have written many authoritative publications on the changes occurring within the energy industry. In their view, empowerment is likely to be the emotional trigger for renewable energy to take off in a much bigger way than economists and purely rational cost-benefit analysis would have us believe. We are part of a virtuous cycle: empowerment leads to more people switching to renewable energy supplies, that accelerates greater decentralisation of power generation, that results in more empowerment locally. Residents in many cities already have the option of switching to renewables but have not done so yet; they can speed up this cycle by changing energy suppliers.

By now it is conventional wisdom that switching to renewable energy supplies is one of the most important steps we need to take to reduce carbon emissions. Achieving the reductions in the Paris Agreement demands that industrialised nations make significant emissions cuts while emerging economies adopt low-carbon pathways. The framework for how different countries should reduce their pollution levels, known as "contraction and convergence", has the virtue of simplicity: equal per capita emissions from everyone. There are no grounds for defending unequal use of the atmosphere. From the inequitable situation we have now, per capita emissions from each country should "converge" at a more even level in the future, while total global emissions should "contract".

What this means in practice depends on where you live. Countries with higher Gross Domestic Product that typically produce higher greenhouse gas emissions need to make greater cuts. Nation states that are already using more of the atmosphere than others include the usual suspects (USA, Russia, China, et al.) as well as those with seemingly better credentials such as Canada and the Scandinavian countries. In practice, it will fall to legacy cities with higher emissions historically to make the cuts while leapfrog cities make less polluting gains. The good news is that cuts do not automatically equate to a lower standard of living for economies that were built on fossil fuels, as there is plenty of evidence that reducing harmful emissions can be decoupled from the health of local economies. With this aim in mind, a country like the U.K. would need to reduce its per capita emissions overall from its current level of eleven tons of carbon dioxide equivalent per person per year to around one ton per person per year by 2050. This reduction in emissions is so significant that the simplest way to think about this cut for the U.K. is no more fossil fuels.

It is entirely possible to transition the energy system of the U.K. and of other countries to one hundred percent renewables. Professor Mark Jacobson and team have developed individual roadmaps for 139 countries to transform the energy infrastructure each country uses for power generation, transportation, heating and cooling, to one powered by wind, water and solar. The roadmaps envisage eighty percent conversion by 2030 and one hundred percent by 2050. Not only is it feasible for wind, water and solar power to replace fossil fuel power but there is also a huge dividend for doing so. Overall energy demand is reduced (by over forty percent globally!) as a result of the switch, in part because extra energy is no longer wasted in extracting, transporting and processing fossil fuels. A huge energy efficiency bonus that far outweighs the cost of anachronistic fossil fuel subsidies.

The mix of renewable energy supplies in each roadmap is just one of many potential combinations of wind, water and solar power that can result in a stable, low-cost system of energy production, distribution and use. The main electricity-generating technologies are already commercially available: onshore and offshore wind turbines, concentrated solar power, geothermal heat and electricity, rooftop and utility-scale solar photovoltaics. The main electric technologies to replace the equivalent fossil fuel technologies are also commercialised on a large scale today, such as electric heat pumps for air and water heating, electric passenger vehicles, electric induction furnaces, electric arc furnaces, dielectric heaters. A few of the electric technologies included are still being designed for commercial use, such as current early stage electric aircraft and hybrid hydrogen fuel cell-electric aircraft, with the assumption that they would be ready for large-scale deployment before 2050.

This research is consistent with conclusions in previous studies: it is technically and economically feasible to transition to renewable energy for all uses; the main barriers are social and political. Citizens can use their power locally to break this logjam, by choosing renewable energy wherever it is available and pushing their city to supply them with cleaner energy where it is not. As researchers Burger and Weinmann have observed in Germany, producing energy locally generates more than a much-needed financial return for city coffers:

Energy moves away from an abstract flow of invisible particles to an issue of personalized identification. As much as locally harvested food is more satisfying for consumers than apples and strawberries produced in a different hemisphere and transported across oceans, locally produced electricity and heat offer the notion of self-determination and ecological consciousness.

In 2013, Hamburg became the largest city in Germany to buy back its energy services. The earlier privatisation of its energy distribution grids for electricity, gas and district heating blocked the ability of local residents to influence further changes, and led to the "Our Hamburg, Our Grid" initiative. According to campaigners at the time, the issue quickly became a "matter of the heart" and a proxy to tackle climate change more effectively by achieving direct access to their energy. Despite the complexity of the topic, at a more visceral level the majority of Hamburg's residents believe that their city's energy services are something for the common good. And this German city is not alone in its desire for greater autonomy over its clean energy supply: over the last ten years 170 municipalities across the country have brought their energy services back into public hands.

At stake is not necessarily the legal ownership of the energy provider but the sense of ownership that comes from citizens having a much greater say in how and where their energy is produced. Some cities take over the ownership of their energy supplies, while others work in partnership with progressive providers. Nonetheless, each city will rely on a unique mix of renewable energy sources, as each geography and topology is different. The relative merits of various eco-technologies are local decisions and the trade-offs are for people on the ground to make. The technical challenge in switching to renewables is not so much in choosing the appropriate mix but in managing a supply that inherently fluctuates: the electricity grid cannot store energy and so production and consumption must be equal all the time.

David MacKay has a wonderfully prosaic, no nonsense approach to such energy supply and demand challenges, and relished replacing ill-informed opinion with realistic numbers in his book, *Sustainable Energy Without the Hot Air*. He looked at fluctuations in our renewable energy in two ways: short-term changes in either energy supply or demand that result in a slew of delivered power, and longer-term lulls when there is little renewable production. In the U.K., for example, the slew rate when a strong wind stops blowing is no worse than in the mornings when everyone gets up, turns on the lights, and switches on the kettle. His point is that short-term fluctuations from renewables are a problem just like the problem of demand spikes that engineers have already solved. Similarly long-term lulls can be addressed either by reducing demand during the entire period or by storing up the energy before the lull (or some combination). Again, the numbers stack up if the grid is smart enough to manage demand and to connect storage systems to the grid.

A storage system near Jamestown in South Australia made the news in December 2017 as the world's largest lithium-ion battery park to date, installed in less than one hundred days and connected to the local Hornsdale wind farm. The one hundred megawatt battery park has storage capacity equivalent to powering over thirty thousand homes for one hour and is compact, taking up the size of twenty basketball courts. The battery is charged from the nearby wind farm when power is plentiful and cheap, and provides top-up power during periods of high-energy demand whether the wind is blowing or not. It is only part of an emerging system of more secure and stable energy, but the physiological impact of reliable renewable power supply and storage is huge for a South Australian population that suffers repeatedly from energy blackouts.

A patchwork of renewable energy solutions is needed to be self-sufficient, so it would be a trap to highlight a single, municipal technology without also mentioning an equally important, scalable disruption led by individuals. The transition to decentralised energy could convert us from passive consumers of energy into active producers. In Germany, for example, more than half of the installed capacity of renewable energy belongs to private owners and farmers, while local utilities and large energy companies have a share of less than twenty percent. Balancing fluctuating supply with inelastic demand can be done even more efficiently in a city where individuals who are producing electricity are concentrated and using storage devices in their homes.

Another decentralised storage solution available in the near future could be the batteries of individuals' electric vehicles that would be designed to avoid the adverse effects of quick and repeated charging. With the advent of improved battery technology, vehicle owners could actively participate in the electricity market by plugging into smart chargers when parked that would charge or draw power based on their household needs and the local electricity demand.

In economist speak, decentralised energy produces positive system externalities. In plain English, this means that the whole is worth more than the sum of its parts. The traditional model of central energy generation is based on optimising a single technology such as a coal-fired power plant, and then creating economies of scale by building on a large scale with an electricity grid that can transport and distribute the energy near and far to where we live and work. In contrast, the model for decentralised energy generation relies on integrating many smaller energy producers – including individual residents and separate neighbourhoods – to form a viable system with different technologies and scales, creating economies of scope within a much more dynamic network. With the focus on multiple producers and a smart electricity grid, instead of large-scale technologies and dumb transmission, individuals and discrete storage services can benefit more easily by plugging into a network. The result is that local energy management diffuses further and further into the heart of urban centres where demand is concentrated.

When the motivation for cleaner energy and more local influence is not purely financial, there are more opportunities for citizens to push for higher standards that set the model for others to follow. This ratcheting up of regulatory standards towards the level of the higher-regulating municipalities is a well-recognised phenomenon known as the "California effect" (after the pattern of adoption by U.S. states of more advanced environmental regulatory standards that originated in California). Put simply, local power can have a much bigger ripple effect than locals envisage.

Unfortunately the grids that distribute electricity to legacy cities were not constructed for transmitting fluctuating energies from different sources. High-voltage lines have to be upgraded to transport renewable energy from more remote sources such as offshore wind farms to urban areas. Medium- and low-voltage lines have to be strengthened to distribute additional energy flows from local sources such as solar panels installed in residential neighbourhoods. Leapfrog cities can avoid the significant expense of expanding a grid-connected energy infrastructure in need of reinforcement by encouraging a more modern, decentralised approach to generating and storing energy. Burger and Weinmann highlight the pitfall of blindly following predecessors:

Massive investments into the central grid could be avoided by extending the storage systems. Once storage systems are in place, the reinforcement of the existing grid would not make sense any longer. A substantial misallocation of resources may take place due to the wrong regulatory incentives. At present, the sequence of the steps undertaken to enhance the energy transformation is not properly balanced: we start by strengthening the grids, but in the long term, less and less electricity will be transmitted.

Nairobi uses half of Kenya's power and is a great example of a city where residents follow their own path in using cleaner energy. The city gets around eighty-five percent of its total electricity supply from a mix of hydro, solar and geothermal. Hell's Gate National Park is named after the intense geothermal activity within the park and is only seventy-five kilometres away, close enough for the capital to access. Cities like Nairobi and Reykjavik are fortunate enough geologically to have access to a naturally occurring source of heat that is close to the surface with good water supply and rock permeability. A "black swan" that could revolutionise the renewable energy industry would be the ability for residents in other cities that are not so lucky to tap into the local supply of geothermal energy under their feet.

The aim of "enhanced geothermal systems" is to use the Earth's underground heat in a significantly wider range of locations where more commonly there is no naturally occurring steam or hot water, and where the permeability of the rock is low. It is a new approach in early stages of commercialisation that draws geothermal power from hot, dry rock sites beneath the ground by pumping high-pressure cold water down an injection well into the rock. Pre-existing joints in the rock create the permeability needed for the fluid to circulate in a closed-loop system, transporting heat back to the surface where electricity can be generated.

Although largely ignored by existing energy markets and government policies, enhanced geothermal systems have the potential to be an important contributor to the energy portfolio as a source of clean, renewable energy. They emit little or no greenhouse gases, can operate outside of traditional hydrothermal areas and function as base load stations producing power twenty-four hours a day with no intermittency, much like a fossil fuel plant. It is interesting to note that Google, a bellwether of big bucks, has its eye on the prize and has invested more money in enhanced geothermal research than the entire U.S. government.

Ironically, the oil and gas industry has extensive drilling experience and expertise that could be deployed to accelerate enhanced geothermal drilling. In the USA, for example, there are over one thousand drilling rigs of which perhaps a dozen are geothermal. Big Oil routinely drills wells of more than eighteen thousand feet (over five kilometres) that would unlock access to geothermal energy for many municipal utilities around the world. Intriguingly, as some oil majors flirt with the idea of becoming utilities, they could be co-opted instead of ostracised, providing services by drilling for renewable geothermal energy. However, we cannot afford to wait for this technology or for their enlightenment, as change starts with us and not with the supermajors.

This newfound attitude towards taking back control is the antithesis of NIMBY ("Not In My Back Yard") opposition, characterised by locals' resistance to any new development close to where they live. Our future energy supply will be more diverse, distributed and downtown. Signs of eco-technology – from wind turbines to solar panels to future geothermal stations – are signs that we have turned the corner rather than turned our back. Switching energy from coal, oil and gas to renewables is an ascent from centralised, remote planning to decentralised, local control.

Over one hundred cities around the world – from Oslo to Auckland, Nairobi to Brasilia – are already mostly powered by renewable energy, sourcing at least seventy percent of their electricity from renewable sources. This figure has doubled in two years as more cities decarbonise more of their electricity supply. Over forty cities worldwide are entirely powered by clean energy, and the ambition of others to follow is growing.

Nonetheless, this industry revolution will not happen fast enough without our active involvement. Public participation is increasingly important: we are the ones choosing our energy supply; we are the ones becoming energy producers, by choice or through necessity where there is no grid. It is a matter of self-determination, not an issue of restructuring traditional utility companies. We want empowerment and more autonomy over our energy supply, for the deeply rooted and emotional reason that it is one of our essential needs.

The origin of energy is an important part of citizenship because it is inextricably linked to creating a better living environment for all members in a community. We start from the heart, by being more vocal and adamant in wanting renewable energy. We take action in our homes, by switching to cleaner energy and ultimately by generating and storing energy. We reduce the risk to our savings, by divesting from oil and gas companies that keep us on the path of climate destruction and whose future value is undercut by our future values.

PROCRASTINATION

One story of Nasreddin, a satirical wise man from the thirteenth century, tells of the time when he lost a precious ring. When his wife asks why he is searching for the ring outside when he lost it in his room, he replies that the room is too dark to see and the light is much better outside. Looking to swap one non-renewable fuel for another is like looking for something where the search is easiest. We will not find the solution there, when what we are really seeking are supplies of renewable energy. Natural gas, "clean coal" and nuclear power all have their advocates for filling the supposed gaps in our energy demand as we make the transition to an emissions-free future. For different reasons all three move in the wrong direction. As energy consumers and influencers, we should be wary of energy policies that do not empower citizens with local energy solutions or go far enough in mitigating greenhouse gas emissions.

The good news is that natural gas has half the carbon dioxide emissions of coal. The bad news is that natural gas has half the carbon dioxide emissions of coal. To serve as a bridge, natural gas must replace coal entirely (a transition that is already happening) and then itself be replaced entirely by renewables (or else the bridge leads to nowhere).

In places like the U.K. where eighty percent of homes are heated by natural gas, this bridging fuel may take longer to go away. However, there are degrees of environmental damage caused by extracting natural gas, with fracking for shale gas undoubtedly being the worst so far. Nations such as the USA have pushed domestic shale gas production in efforts to switch from imports, for energy security reasons rather than as a clean alternative to dirty coal. The stampede has been so strong that almost two-thirds of natural gas production in the USA now comes from shale gas fracking.

The blackened bandwagon has gathered pace. Canada became the next frontier for shale gas, eager to emulate its big brother. China and other nations joined in, as governments hustled to boost their domestic supply of non-renewable energy. Considering this push for more natural gas in the larger context of lowering emissions, and its future replacement, sets two alarm bells ringing loudly: fracking for new supplies of shale gas is not much better for the climate than burning coal; building long-term natural gas infrastructure is not economically feasible if natural gas is going to be replaced.

Opposition to fracking comes from all sides: the use of carcinogenic chemicals that cause water and land contamination; the huge volumes of water transported to fracking sites at significant environmental cost; and the seismic activity induced by fracturing deep-rock formations in order for natural gas and petroleum to flow more freely. To cap it all, methane, that otherwise stays underground, is emitted during fracking when natural gas escapes unburned, and at much higher rates than previously understood. Invisible and odourless, methane seeps out from the pipes, welds, joints and valves across the entire natural gas infrastructure, and especially when connected to operations that involve exploding rock to open up new holes. It even leaks from assumed sealed wells as the cement poured into the wells by the frackers shrinks when it solidifies, leaving gaps for the gas to continue escaping. Hissing in the background, this greenhouse gas is pernicious. It is more than eighty times as potent as carbon dioxide and takes up to twenty years to dissipate.

Local resistance is increasing as fracking moves closer to where people live and its harm becomes ever more apparent to more people. Over one million people live within five miles of the largest urban oil field in the USA, in Los Angeles County at the Inglewood oil field. The site's productivity had declined steadily until the oil company started fracking to extract the remaining petroleum reserves that were inaccessible through more conventional drilling methods. The practice went mostly unnoticed by local residents until a fracking accident at the oil field released a cloud of toxic fumes that forced the evacuation of some neighbourhood areas. After the accident and resulting protest, more stringent drilling regulations were enforced within the city limits to address legitimate health and safety concerns.

Fort Worth in Texas is home to 740,000 people and is perhaps the epicentre of urban fracking. The city is home to over two thousand natural gas wells, with some less than two hundred metres away from homes, schools and parks. The city has toughened its own municipal rules in an attempt to regulate land use better and defend the quality of life of Fort Worthers, but the city is closing the barn door after the horse has bolted. Fort Worth is a shocking example of how the fracking industry can encroach upon the lives of communities one well at a time, and a wake-up call for residents in other cities not immune to its advances.

The lock-in of natural gas infrastructure does not spell good news either. According to energy and climate expert Michael Levi, who was also a Special Assistant to President Obama for USA Energy and Economic Policy, global natural gas consumption would have to peak around 2020 to 2030 in order to limit global warming below two degrees Celsius. The natural gas infrastructure built in recent years will barely have time to break even, let alone generate profits. It is apparent that most of these new assets would be stranded in the future if emissions reductions become binding. To square the circle, some argue that natural gas infrastructure could continue operating in a carbon-neutral world with biofuel and carbon capture and storage technology. This scenario is a pipe dream.

The concept of "clean coal" is more of an idea than a reality. It is not a special type of coal or a new technology that reduces the environmental impact of coal mining. It refers instead to the technology that would treat coal before burning and to carbon capture and storage technology that would clean up the emissions from burning coal. The captured carbon would then be buried in geological formations where it would stay trapped. However, clean coal increases the cost of conventional coal-fired power at the same time as renewable power alternatives become cheaper, even without the support of subsidies. As a 2015 report by London's Overseas Development Institute explains:

To capture carbon dioxide at a power station requires adding a large separation unit, which also requires a significant amount of power to run. Adding the extra process currently doubles the capital costs of a plant, while running the separation process effectively decreases the overall efficiency of the plant by around a quarter... From the U.S. to South Africa to India, new unsubsidised renewable power is already competitive with conventional coal-fired power.

The technology itself has been very slow to develop and hence why it is being overtaken by renewables. It still has uncertainties regarding the underground storage of carbon dioxide, the ineffectiveness of capturing other greenhouse gases, and the scale and cost to implement. When left in the ground, coal naturally stores the carbon that has already been pulled out of the atmosphere by plants. In truth, most of this coal must remain *in situ* as it is the only proven way we know of storing carbon underground. Cities already have cleaner energy alternatives than the promise of clean coal; carbon capture and storage is not an investment we should bank on. According to the authors of an assessment report by the Overseas Development Institute:

Even if carbon capture and storage were now technologically and commercially proven and available, 82% of known coal reserves would not be burnable between now and 2050 [if we are to stay below the dangerous 2°C threshold]. Perhaps even more importantly, because of the production of further hydrocarbons, there are significant questions over the level of emissions abated.

The elephant in the room is nuclear power. Love it or hate it, nuclear polarises opinion. David MacKay outlines the unique property of nuclear power: the nuclear energy available per atom is roughly one million times bigger than the chemical energy per atom of typical fuels. As a result, the amounts of fuel and waste that must be dealt with at a nuclear reactor can be up to one million times smaller than those at an equivalent fossil-fuel power station. Nuclear plants also have a high efficiency and generate a stable supply of power so that they deliver a constant base load in comparison to intermittent renewables. And even though it is not a renewable energy supply, the greenhouse gas emissions are low when the plant is operational.

Despite these benefits, the share of nuclear power within the overall mix of electricity generation worldwide has declined over the last twenty years and is expected to continue. The meltdown at the Fukushima nuclear reactor in 2011 has cast a long shadow over the entire nuclear power industry, dispersing even more radiation into the environment than the Chernobyl catastrophe in Russia. Nations like Japan and France that rely heavily on nuclear energy have reassessed their long-term commitment to this energy supply. The most immediate reversal came from Germany, when Chancellor Angela Merkel announced within days of the nuclear disaster in Japan that Germany would gradually turn off all nuclear power plants forever.

Nuclear power is not as carbon-free as it first appears. Greenhouse gases are emitted during the initial stages of uranium mining, conversion of uranium ore, fuel enrichment and reactor construction. At the end of the cycle, more greenhouse gases are emitted during reactor decommissioning, fuel reprocessing, nuclear waste disposal and site rehabilitation. In the commissioning phase nuclear represents an opportunity cost relative to wind, water and solar energy in terms of the long time lag from planning application to plant operation. For example, a wind farm typically takes two to five years to be up and running, whereas a nuclear plant takes up to twenty years and burns vast quantities of fossil fuels over that extended period.

However, the biggest detractor of nuclear power is not the time it takes to become operational or all the hidden carbon emissions, but the real and perceived risks. The Intergovernmental Panel on Climate Change concluded in its *Fifth Assessment Report*:

Barriers to and risks associated with an increasing use of nuclear energy include operational risks and the associated safety concerns, uranium mining risks, financial and regulatory risks, unresolved waste management issues, nuclear weapons proliferation concerns, and adverse public opinion.

Advanced nuclear power designs, such as integral fast reactors and thorium accelerator-driven systems, cannot be evaluated properly until they have moved from technological demonstrations to commercial deployment. Nonetheless, they will still have some of the same perceived risks associated with nuclear power that the public and governments share, including meltdown accidents, waste storage and disposal, and the risk of the use of nuclear technology in weapons.

The density of demand means major cities can never be fully self-sufficient in energy, even if energy usage is reduced and more renewable energy is generated within the city limits. For those living in bigger cities, it is not even close; for example, around ninety-four percent of London's energy demand is currently sourced from outside the city boundaries. The push by citizens for cleaner energy is inextricably linked to their nation's energy policies and the decarbonisation of electricity supply. Although we do not decide national energy policies, we can directly influence the long-term decisions about bridging fuels by the speed with which we adopt renewable energy and turn our backs on fossil fuels.

The cost of procrastination is not simply a delay in what needs to be done, but a cost in doing something else that needs to be undone. If we are to transition successfully to renewable energy, we should press home our demands, and cities should address the more immediate gaps in smarter electricity grids, regional and micro-grids, and local energy storage solutions. We will not find what we are looking for in shale gas, clean coal or nuclear: they are bridges that lead to nowhere.

RESOURCEFULNESS

You do not need to look far to see the volume of household waste put out on the street for collection; the dumpsters filled to the brim by residents living in apartments and condos; the garbage piled up on roadsides. Fleets of garbage trucks operate every day of the year just to keep up. This detritus has become a curse of our own making. An estimated seventy-eight billion tons of raw materials entered the global economy in 2018, most of it heading straight out the other end in a growing flow of waste. We are drowning, no longer able to stay on top of this accumulation.

In a circular world, waste is recognised as unrealised energy that has not yet been converted into something more useful. If we remake our economies so that resources go round instead of pass through, resources are used for as long as possible, maximum value is extracted from them while in use, and materials are recovered or products regenerated at the end of their service life. In doing so we address overshoot, at the core of our ecological crisis.

The circular flow of materials is inherently profitable and the potential gains largely untapped today. It is a radically better system from a material consumption and emissions point of view, and its impact is fundamental to a future restorative economy. The concept is not a new one and its origins date back to the 1970s. Since then we have made progress on renewable energy and energy efficiency, but too little has been done to reduce the massive damage we cause in the process of extracting natural resources from the Earth and then dumping the finished products. It is high time to stem the flow of new materials.

If we revisit *The Limits to Growth* – that prescient report forecasting how the world was moving too fast in the wrong direction – the limits to endless economic growth boil down to depleting raw materials too quickly and creating pollution from discarding too much waste. Unfortunately demand calls forth supply, as economists would say. The problem is that new technology and innovation continue to push the limitations on supply further into the future. We keep finding more oil and more minerals, inventing new materials, consuming more stuff. Hence the report's dire prediction that Earth's capacity to absorb our pollution would inevitably be exceeded if we continued to discard increasing volumes of materials and chemicals as unwanted waste. This warning has always been the most powerful part of *The Limits to Growth*.

A fundamental reorganisation of the way we produce, consume and cycle resources could support our entire urbanised population, but it calls for "circular economies" that work because we keep resources in use for as long as possible instead of chasing the next shiny new thing. Some of the systemic changes we need to make include focusing on usage rather than ownership, widespread dematerialising, and recycling. By its very nature, operating within a circular economy reduces the waste we produce, reduces the environmental impacts of production and consumption, and reduces the demand for new stuff – without reversing prosperity. Apparently we can have our cake and eat it, provided we know when we are full. This is only possible when we start thinking and behaving more resourcefully. When we believe there is no such thing as waste. When we sacrifice glut for sufficiency, and choose to do more with less.

Shifting to a circular economy requires change at all levels, from citizens to countries, and from cities to companies. As places where consumption is most concentrated, cities amplify the demands and pressures but are also uniquely placed to lead the transition. An exemplary "circular city" includes a built environment that minimises the use of new raw materials, is highly utilised by residents based on shared spaces, and by design preserves energy, water and food. It relies on renewable energy for its power, an efficient integrated transport system for its mobility, and a bio-economy for some of its food. It also has thriving circular economies for local production, repairing and distributive manufacturing, and diverse exchanges of goods, materials and services.

Sounds too improbable to happen? Residents, enterprises and the municipal government in Amsterdam are leading the way when it comes to the real work of inventing a circular city. The *Circular Innovation Programme* is full of creative ways that Amsterdammers are reducing, recycling and reusing materials, from buildings that can be taken apart and reassembled elsewhere to leasing washing machines instead of buying them to growing useful chemicals.

The crown jewel is perhaps the Amsterdam district of Buiksloterham, intended to be fully circular by 2025. The neighbourhood is a former industrial waterfront that was home to an aeroplane factory, oil refinery and shipbuilding. An informal group of citizens and planners stepped in when developers pulled out, with a proposal for the neighbourhood to become the model for a new circular economy. The reinvention is well underway, with ongoing public workshops involving residents and designers being an integral part of this collaborative urbanism.

In a detailed report entitled *Circular Buiksloterham* these city-making locals have outlined their vision for the neighbourhood. It is far-reaching and includes a near full circular material flow, full resource recovery from waste water, fully renewable energy supply, self-renewing ecosystems, zero-emissions for local mobility, and a strong economy that encourages exchanges of social, environmental and cultural services.

Action has turned these ideas into reality. Zero-packaging food co-ops deliver fresh produce to residents twice a week through the local collection point. Residents and businesses recycle everything, from waste cooking oils to plastics to electronics. There have been many community tree-planting schemes, and almost half of all buildings have some form of green roof or green wall for water buffering. At the bidding of residents, all buildings have multi-functional roofs for both energy generation and water retention. "Time banking" has opened up a dynamic, parallel economy where citizens trade skills in addition to exchanging money. This local service not only provides an essential exchange of expertise between local residents but also strengthens community and civic participation.

Emerging companies and entrepreneurs are filling gaps in the circular flow of materials and making healthy profits from operations that are no longer niche. In Buiksloterham, for example, "new industrial" businesses like Urbania (Europe's first urban mining centre), 3DPrintery (on-demand manufacturing) and ReTex (a local fashion hub using only remanufactured and recycled textiles) play an integral role in closing urban material cycles as well as providing new jobs. At the same time, existing companies recognise the need to evolve, by designing out waste, implementing product-to-service strategies and innovating with more collaborative business models. Those companies located in more progressive cities with nascent circular economies will have a competitive advantage; those in less dynamic cities can take the lead. Companies that have grown up with linear production systems or do not have deep roots locally cannot afford to ignore these new profit opportunities – they have too much to gain rather than too much to lose.

Companies also provide platforms for locals to sell or rent unused products or spare service capacity, without the need for the company itself to own the assets that are shared. It is no longer a surprise to us that the world's largest taxi firm (Uber) owns no cars, the largest provider of accommodation (Airbnb) owns no property, or the largest retailer (Alibaba) carries no stock. Instead of conventionally selling products, other companies offer "products as a service" whereby customers pay for the time or usage of a product while the company retains ownership throughout its entire lifecycle. These assets are utilised better through their reuse and the material flows improved through remanufacturing and recycling. Almost any type of equipment is on offer as a service if we care to look, from vehicles and heavy machinery to office furniture and medical equipment.

We can improve the flow of materials in different ways, by decreasing its volume, slowing down its churn rate or reducing its toxicity. It is challenging, not because it is technically difficult, but because we have to collaborate and cooperate with each other. Citizen-led initiatives can improve material flows by connecting individuals, who have decided to do more to reduce their waste, with local businesses that support environmentally sustainable action, encouraging recycling while strengthening social ties between engaged citizens. Grassroots initiatives work because they not only overturn the entrenched way we throw things away but also create momentum behind new social norms.

The good news and the bad news is that almost every material flow can be improved, provided there is sufficient willpower from participants. The flow of plastics is a case in point as we have become acutely aware of the impact of our plastic waste. The material is not biodegradable, is expensive to recycle effectively, and is polluting if it is burnt, buried or discarded. If we continue to dispose of plastics in the oceans at a similar rate as we do today, by 2050 there will be more plastic in the ocean by weight than fish. Broken down into tiny beads, harmful plastics are ingested by animals and marine life and then in turn by us. If you did not care about the fish eating your plastic before, you might care now that you are eating the plastic in your fish.

The consumer movement for responsible use of plastic is growing exponentially. Industry pressure has increased dramatically as China stopped importing contaminated non-industrial plastic from overseas in 2018 (along with paper products and other low-value garbage). For the last twenty-five years China has been the largest importer of the world's plastics waste, accepting over seventy percent of the total waste exported by other countries. Unfortunately China's change in recycling policy is the result of increased plastic waste domestically that has reduced its dependence on foreign suppliers for business, rather than progressive thinking on the environmental impact of such waste. As a consequence many more cities in Europe, Asia and the Americas have to deal with their own mess – not by dumping it elsewhere but by encouraging less use of plastics in the first place.

Take plastic water bottles in the USA as just one illustration of the flood of plastic materials and the actions that can be taken. Americans used over fifty billion plastic water bottles in 2016, with less than one quarter of those bottles recycled after single use. Although most plastic bottles used for soft drinks and water are made from highly recyclable polyethylene terephthalate (PET), efforts to collect and recycle these bottles are simply not keeping up with usage. Cities such as San Francisco are tackling the issue by ensuring that water is treated as a public good, instead of a commodity sold by companies, prioritising access for all its residents to safe tap water. The city is increasing its investment in public water fountains and water bottle filling stations, and is leading the way by phasing out the sale of single-use plastic water bottles in all city properties.

More than one hundred American cities have adopted similar measures to stem the flow of plastic bottles, restricting government spending on bottled water and extending bans to national parks and universities. Consumer companies can play their part by manufacturing more of their packaging from recycled content and designing out waste, although these efforts to reduce the volume of plastic they produce are offset by their financial targets to increase volume. As consumers we are the problem, but also the solution. We are the ones who can shift the culture back to habits that were common before unnecessary plastic water bottles were produced by the billions. We can choose between the "inconvenience" of drinking from a glass, drinking tap water or drinking from a refillable bottle that we carry with us, and the convenience of discarding yet another plastic bottle after our few sips that takes hundreds of years to decompose.

The suggestion of zero waste may seem more of an ideal than a realistic objective (despite the fact that there is zero waste in nature). In practice, zero waste means that we seek to eliminate all forms of waste, and municipalities seek to divert all waste from landfills by recycling and composting. It means the mantra of "reduce, reuse, recycle" would apply not just to products at the end of their life span, but to the materials and methods used to create them. The path to zero waste might be thought of as an asymptote, forever curving toward its destination: we may never arrive there but we can get as close as possible.

A circular economy is a boon for new, secure jobs. Given all the interactions that can prolong the useful life of materials, being resourceful inevitably involves more people and creates new opportunities that cannot easily be automated. The focus of past industrial revolutions was on labour productivity – producing more stuff with fewer employees – with scant regard for the inefficient use of natural resources or the social cost of unemployment. When the focus turns from the wastefulness with which the economy uses raw materials to cyclical flows, more employees are needed to maintain and refurbish existing products and to support the big shift from product ownership to more flexible access to products as services.

A host of studies all show a positive impact on job creation in the transition to circular cities. The transformation is not simply a one-for-one replacement of jobs in fossil fuel energy with jobs in renewable energy, or from jobs in primary manufacturing to remanufacturing. There is a broader shift in a circular economy from labour-scarce raw material sectors to the more labour-intensive recycling sector. New jobs across different skill levels and pay grades are required, from recycling and reuse to more technical remanufacturing and highly specialised bio-refining. Many of the new jobs are local to the cities where services and people are concentrated and are not threatened by potential offshoring. These "new industrial" jobs require custom work that cannot easily be replaced by robots and can spring up in cities across the country, including hard-hit regions with high unemployment where old industries have declined.

Circular cities increase employment, produce welfare gains and recouple the local economy with the environment. So why is the transition so slow in spite of such obvious benefits? National government plays its part, with policies that are inconsistent with the new direction: economic success is measured principally by the flow-based metric of Gross Domestic Product; billions of dollars of state subsidies for fossil fuels are a drag on positive change; externalities such as carbon emissions are not priced properly and hence there is a lack of true cost and accountability.

Market pressures also play a part, with companies thinking too small: treating waste as a hazard to be disposed of safely rather than as a valuable source of materials and components; optimising linear production systems instead of shifting to cyclical business models; avoiding collaboration with other companies for the sake of narrow and insecure competitive advantage. And last but not least, we play our part in how we respond to the change that is asked of us: making an effort to be more than passive consumers; dispelling the myth that convenience is everything; rethinking our attitude and our behaviour towards buying, using and eventually disposing of all the products around us.

As both citizens and consumers, we create the "pull" on both local government and companies that helps steer circular cities and creates new jobs. We have both the political power to ensure city governments take action and the purchasing power to incentivise the right kinds of suppliers. We have the power to hold onto products for longer, buy fewer products or replace them entirely with services, and support only those brands that promote our values. Like the circular economy itself, ultimately it comes back to us. We are resourceful enough to make things last and to do more with less. Let's pull others along with us.

Saving Life

BIODIVERSITY

Despite the mass human migration from rural to urban areas, we never lost our dependency on nature. Our urban way of life has been built on a foundation of natural resources and is sustained by essential ecosystems. Biodiversity – the variety of plants, animals and microorganisms – provides our basis for life by ensuring we have clean air and water, producing fertile soils and all of our food, making the raw materials for our clothing and medicines, and maintaining functioning ecosystems that supply these and other irreplaceable services.

The idea of ecosystem services has been very influential and is now well established. An ecosystem is a functional unit made up of plant, animal and microorganism communities, interacting with each other and also with their environment. Humans are an integral part of ecosystems. Ecosystems can vary enormously in size: a temporary pond in a storm drain and an ocean basin can both be ecosystems. The many benefits we derive may be grouped together as "provisioning services" such as our supplies of food and fresh water; "supporting services" such as soil formation and nutrient cycling; "regulating services" such as natural protection from coastal storm surges and land degradation; and "cultural services" that we value for spiritual or religious reasons, or for recreational purposes.

Talk of ecosystem services does not stir people's imagination, suggesting instead that nature provides a service like a utility company. Worse still it can perpetuate the myth that humans are in control. Putting a true economic value on many of these services can also be challenging, especially for cultural services – such as inspiration, identity and sense of belonging – that come from the natural environment simply because it exists. It is ironic that we tend to discount most heavily the very services that resonate most deeply within us.

Nature is undeniably valuable in its own right and not simply because it is so useful to us. The notion of protecting biodiversity because it is necessary to maintain essential ecosystem services is plainly a utilitarian kind of environmentalism. Saving nature for its own sake would be a more worthy aim than saving nature to shield us from harm. Nonetheless, the goal of regeneration is still achieved, whether the motivation is to protect other species or simply ourselves. However, we should remain vigilant in adopting an economic perspective, as there is a big difference between the concept of ecosystem services to quantify value and an appreciation of nature that recognises its full worth. The former is a mechanism for pricing and payment; the latter is the more compelling narrative of passion and persuasion.

Our urban population has expanded at the expense of biodiversity. The current extinction rate exceeds our planetary boundary: we are killing too many species too fast for ecosystems to cope. The first imperative of economic restoration cannot be achieved or sustained without ensuring that nature regenerates. Hence the second imperative of civic revolution is to protect biodiversity, a visceral appeal to people's innate feelings for nature and to more humane action.

It might seem counterintuitive that biodiversity is a crucial element for prosperous urban living. What could be less natural than the high concentration of humanity in cities? It would appear more obvious that cities are bad for the environment and that the more pristine environment beyond the city limits should be protected instead. As we shall see when we shift our thinking, those cities (their residents and municipal governments) that wish to survive will be the ones that take the lead on protecting biodiversity within as well as beyond their boundaries. For example, take the soil beneath our feet that we treat no better than dirt, or take sand, our most used natural resource after air and water.

Soil is a living material that consists of organic matter, minerals, gases, liquids and organisms. It is interconnected with other ecosystems, from water to the climate. Estimates based on the current rate of soil degradation around the world suggest that we have about sixty years left – sixty harvests in utilitarian terms – before we run out of usable topsoil. We will no longer be able to supply as much food to cities when soil productivity has been lost and urban water shortages will become more acute as degraded soil retains less than half the water. The consequences for us of this biodiversity loss are profound.

We are running out of sand too, used in everything from glass to paint, computer chips to plastics. Concrete is our main use for sand: a suburban house requires two hundred tons of sand to build; a kilometre of highway takes fifteen thousand tons. Unfortunately we cannot use desert sand, as wind erosion makes the grains too round, so we dredge marine sand. In total we use a staggering fifty billion tons of sand every year, twice the amount produced by every river in the world. Collecting this sand destroys marine habitat and removes the home of microorganisms that feed the base of the food chain. Like the aquatic life that perishes, we take the presence of sand for granted until it is gone.

Another element of biodiversity is plant life that regulates our climate and has the potential to mitigate global warming. Plants take in carbon dioxide by photosynthesis during the day and release carbon dioxide during respiration at night. Plants take up much more carbon dioxide during photosynthesis than they give off in respiration; if left to grow, they fix about twenty times more carbon than is released by fossil fuel combustion. When their photosynthesis outpaces respiration and combustion, the biosphere on land becomes a natural sink for carbon, reducing the rate of carbon dioxide accumulation in the atmosphere. In addition to their vital role in the carbon cycle, plants also regulate change by absorbing and dissipating solar energy at ground level, and modulate the water cycle through plant transpiration.

It is essential to recognise that biodiversity is not incompatible with urban life; indeed it already exists within all cities. For example, Warsaw is home to around sixty-five percent of all bird species in Poland; Berlin has twenty-two habitats of global importance. While intact natural habitats hold the richest biodiversity, urban habitats are surprisingly diverse – ranging from traditional agricultural land on the edges of human settlement to the urban-industrial landscapes made up of residential neighbourhoods, industrial areas, city parks and brownfields. Some urban sites that provide habitats are remnants of native vegetation such as the bushland in Sydney and Perth or the Sonoran desert parks in Tucson and Phoenix. Other sites are protected because of their cultural heritage or long history of non-usage, from the evergreen forests of the Botanical Garden in Singapore to the Atlantic rainforests of the Mata Atlantica in Rio de Janeiro.

The wealth of urban biodiversity is influenced by the condition of the original ecosystems. Many cities are located in biodiversity-rich areas – on floodplains, river estuaries and along coastlines – where the abundance of life favoured the locations for settlement and from where cities grew. The economic, social and cultural values of citizens in these urban areas today will determine the future of this biodiversity. Deliberate care and integration can protect these remnant natural assets by conserving the native ecosystems within the city. For example, the world's first National City Park comprises twenty-seven square kilometres right in the middle of the metropolitan area of Stockholm; wildlife is diverse and prolific in Table Mountain National Park, protected and surrounded by the municipality of Cape Town; over one hundred square kilometres of semi-evergreen forests thrive in Sanjay Gandhi National Park, entirely within the megacity of Mumbai.

Natural ecosystems in urban areas are known to have positive effects on our wellbeing. They provide places for relaxation, recreation and community cohesion. People who interact and reconnect with nature in their city renew their appreciation of the broader environment. Access for city residents to green areas has been linked to reduced mortality and improvements in their general health. Despite all the research to date, we still have not discovered or fully comprehended the breadth and depth of nature's impact on urban living. The danger from our lack of understanding is that we undervalue its true worth and behave accordingly.

In the next chapter we look at a host of benefits derived from just one example, urban trees, to illustrate the priceless nature of biodiversity on a scale that is easier to imagine. This focus is not intended to overlook the connectivity between different elements within nature: it seeks instead to bring this web to life. Cities are immersed in nature's web of interconnected systems and flows: like everywhere else, they are impacted by the health of the subsoil, biosphere and atmosphere. If we choose to reinvent the role of greenery within our cities, then naturally other elements will follow. To quote Maja Lunde, novelist and author of *The History of Bees*, "Everything is connected to everything, it's as simple and difficult as that."

For most people today, the loss of biodiversity is seen as less urgent than other immediate pressures in urban life, something separate and less important than issues related to poverty or housing or sanitation. This perception is misguided: healthy ecosystems underlie all aspects of urban development and vitality, either directly or indirectly. We need to think very differently about how we treat the role of biodiversity within our lives, and go well beyond the traditional ideas of conservation of pristine ecosystems. Ingenious new approaches are required in how we live with nature that embed as well as mimic natural solutions to alleviate the pressures of urban living. With contributions from more than 120 scientists and policy-makers around the world, the *Cities and Biodiversity Outlook* report adds:

Cities already represent a new class of ecosystems shaped by the dynamic interactions between ecological and social systems. As we project the spread of these ecosystems across the globe, we must become more proactive in trying not only to preserve components of earlier ecosystems and services that they displace, but in imagining and building entirely new kinds of ecosystems that allow for a reconciliation between human development and biodiversity.

Our personal health is inextricably linked to the health of biodiversity, and our bad habits ruin more than our own health. People make vibrant cities, but not on their own. For we cannot live in cities independently of nature: our dependency on nature enables us to live in cities. We need to show ingenuity in working with nature, and initiative in working for nature, if we are to be resilient and our cities to endure.

INGENUITY

The benefits of green infrastructure are hidden in plain sight. The biodiversity within a "city canopy" is uniquely important to urban living, by maintaining and improving our quality of life in ways that cannot be manufactured. If left unloved, this living infrastructure does not have long to live. Unless local residents defend green spaces that come under commercial pressures, or advocate growing them in the face of budget cuts, they wither away. Encouragingly, there are countless environmental volunteer projects that improve city neighbourhoods, from restoring brownfield land to conserving water to improving air quality. City residents and entrepreneurs are also taking the initiative locally to produce food, with innovative approaches to urban agriculture from allotments to planting fruit and vegetables on rooftops. Some citizens have gone further by growing these grassroots community projects into movements, such as the Transition Network, with its aim of increasing self-sufficiency and building resilience in urban areas through transition initiatives such as local food production.

The nature of any city canopy depends on the particular geography, climate and topology, and varies by place from parks to scrublands, riverbanks to dry arroyos, vegetable gardens to tree-lined boulevards. Far from an ornamental afterthought, the city canopy is a core element of healthy urban living. Consider trees as one example of the benefits of urban biodiversity. Before elaborating on the advantages we gain from the presence of trees, we should first pause to appreciate their astonishing nature. The subtitle of Peter Wohllenben's book, The Hidden Life of Trees, is incredibly, "What They Feel, How They Communicate". As a forester with decades of study and observation he brings new understanding to the biggest plants on the planet.

What are some of the unexpected ways he has discovered that trees communicate with animals and other trees? If insects are eating its leaves, a tree sends airborne chemical signals that attract predators that feed on that specific insect. Even more surprisingly, if a grazing animal is eating its leaves the tree sends different chemical signals to other trees warning them of the threat. Neighbouring trees respond by releasing toxic chemicals to deter that animal from moving on to them.

In a forest, trees also share sugars and other nutrients underground to keep each other healthy, and share information about their environment through a far-reaching web of soil fungi. In urban areas, streets and pathways that have been planted with rows of the same species of tree enable individual trees to communicate and support each other in a similar fashion. Why do they do this? Because a forest of healthy trees creates a microclimate suitable for all the trees in the vicinity to grow. Wohllenben goes on to observe:

Hence isolated trees do not live as long as those living connected together in forests. Forests are super-organisms with interconnections much like ant colonies. In the symbiotic community of the forest, not only trees but also shrubs and grasses – and possibly all plant species – exchange information in this way.

There are a few species of tree, including poplars and silver birches, which forego the social interactions and support of a forest and grow alone, intending to colonise new areas in the process. They defend themselves by growing quickly, putting on a massive layer of rough outer bark. Birch bark, for example, also contains betulin, a healing compound with antiviral and antibacterial properties, enabling single birches to be more self-reliant.

Trees that live on streets lead tough lives. They have restricted space, endure a hot urban microclimate that they cannot control, and are up against an impermeable asphalt surface and compacted subsoil that do not readily let water get to their roots. Growing on the side of roads and street corners, they receive unwanted doses of salt in the winter and acidic urine from dogs year round. They lead shorter lives than their relatives in the wild, dying prematurely from the stresses of their environment. Nonetheless, city trees still give back to the plants, animals and people around them; and the longer they live the more we all benefit. In the cities where they grow, street trees have in them the natural power to:

IMPROVE AIR QUALITY

Air pollution is one of the leading preventable causes of death in the world, killing nearly seven million people a year mostly in urban areas. About a quarter of deaths from heart disease, stroke and lung cancer can be attributed to air pollution, according to the World Health Organisation. Urban trees remove gaseous air pollutants by uptake through their leaves as well as by intercepting airborne particles. Large trees are much more effective than smaller ones: researchers have calculated that a tree with ten times the trunk diameter removes approximately seventy times more air pollution annually. In urban areas with contiguous tree cover the overall improvements in air quality from pollution removal by trees were as high as fifteen percent for ozone, fourteen percent for sulphur dioxide and thirteen percent for particulate matter.

REDUCE URBAN HEAT ISLAND EFFECTS

Higher average temperatures from climate change intensify the higher ambient temperatures in urban areas compared to rural areas, known as the "urban heat island effect". This effect is most intense at night as man-made heat emissions combine with buildings and roads that absorb more solar radiation than green vegetation during the day. Urban parks and vegetation reduce the urban heat island effect. Data from Manchester, U.K., showed that a ten percent increase in tree cover resulted in a three degree Celsius drop in urban temperatures.

PROTECT FROM STORM WATER

Extensive areas of impermeable surfaces in urban areas result in large volumes of surface water runoff and increase urban vulnerability to the increased frequency and intensity of storms. Interception of rainfall by trees, other vegetation, and permeable soils in urban areas can be critical in reducing the pressure on drainage systems and lowering the risk of surface water flooding. According to *Cities and Biodiversity Outlook*, urban landscapes with fifty to ninety percent impervious ground cover can lose up to eighty percent of incoming rainfall to surface runoff, whereas forested landscapes lose only about thirteen percent in similar storms.

IMPROVE HUMAN HEALTH

Urban trees can be thought of as public health infrastructure as they deliver measurable mental and physical health benefits to concrete-fatigued city residents. For example, in New York City where asthma is the leading cause of hospitalisation among children under age fifteen, researchers at Columbia University studied the correlation between numbers of trees on residential streets and incidences of childhood asthma. They found that as the number of trees rose, the prevalence of childhood asthma fell, even after the data were adjusted for socio-demographics, population density and proximity to pollution sources. A recent report by The Nature Conservancy went further by proposing a novel way of linking the goals and funding of the health sector with urban tree planting, in order to close the investment gap in trees for quantifiable health reasons.

INCREASE BIODIVERSITY

Trees play an important role in increasing urban biodiversity, providing plants and animals with a favourable habitat, food and protection. Less obvious is the invisible contribution of trees to the urban microbiome. Just as scientists have started to realise that the bacteria in our gut play a major role in our health, so the teeming microbes in city air are also intrinsic to our wellbeing. The issue is that the built environment seals and sterilises our living spaces, makes us more prone. The microbes in the air over a concrete expanse differ from the microbes over green spaces, and we are discovering unsurprisingly that those over green spaces are the ones we should be breathing.

SOAK UP ATMOSPHERIC CARBON

Stopping the increase of carbon dioxide in the atmosphere is not enough to meet the target of keeping global warming below two degrees Celsius. Emissions cannot be cut fast enough to keep the stock of greenhouse gases below this threshold level – unless carbon is actually taken out of the air. Over one hundred of the 116 scenarios that the Intergovernmental Panel on Climate Change have analysed involve carbon removal schemes. The median scenario assumes that a total of 810 billion tons of carbon dioxide are extracted from the atmosphere before 2100. That is the equivalent of extracting around twenty years of global emissions at our current levels.

Outlandish ideas such as sucking up carbon directly from the air using chemical filters or sowing vast quantities of alkaline minerals in the oceans to absorb more carbon dioxide are no better than other dangerous geoengineering proposals. The hard truth is that "negative emissions technologies" do not exist on the large scale needed for scrubbing carbon from the air, and waiting for a new carbon sink to be invented is a moral hazard. Business magnate Richard Branson's prize of twenty-five million dollars to the first person to invent a "commercially viable design" that would remove one billion tons of greenhouse gases a year for ten years has gone unclaimed, for over ten years.

Plants are nature's solution to a negative emissions technology. While they are growing, trees use sunlight to absorb carbon dioxide from the atmosphere through photosynthesis and store it as carbon in the form of wood. Younger trees absorb carbon dioxide quickly while they are growing, but a steady state is eventually reached when the amount of carbon absorbed through photosynthesis is similar to that lost through respiration and decay. If new trees are planted near this time in the growth cycle, then we can maintain trees as a net sink of carbon. Given the scale of climate change, the challenge in adopting nature's solution is the amount of land needed for afforestation. In an urbanised world where land is being used for settlement, we need to be inventive in creating large areas for tree growing within cities and in peri-urban regions.

Vertical construction has proven to be an efficient way of creating more homes and offices while keeping the footprint relatively small, with buildings rising into the sky rather than spreading along the ground. This precedent has been applied in Milan, where the Milanese have expanded their urban green space by creating two "vertical forests". Not far from the busy Garibaldi train station, a couple of residential tower blocks have been covered in eight hundred trees, five thousand shrubs and fifteen thousand plants. If all these plants were in the ground instead of in the sky, they would cover twenty thousand square metres.

Similar projects have been commissioned in Switzerland, the Netherlands and China, as other cities take up the lead. The most ambitious proposal is Chinese, where the Liuzhou Forest City will have seventy buildings cascading with foliage. This new town will be home to thirty thousand people, with buildings covered by forty thousand trees and one million plants. A forward-thinking city where trees outnumber people. These vertical forests are expected to absorb almost ten thousand tons of carbon dioxide and fifty-seven tons of pollutants per year.

Such ingenuity is not the exclusive domain of visionary architects or progressive city planners. Residents can be ingenious too, by creating improvised vertical forests on the balconies of apartment buildings. Championed by a few individuals within the building, coordinated action creates a façade that absorbs carbon dioxide and other airborne toxins. In buildings without balconies, residents get together instead to grow vibrant roof gardens and parklets in the sky.

Unfortunately the connection between disengaged citizens and declining green infrastructure is all too common. In the USA, for example, despite the strong evidence of the environmental and health benefits of urban trees and their strategic importance, urban trees are steadily disappearing. According to The Nature Conservancy, around four million urban trees die or disappear each year in the USA without being replaced, even though studies quantify that every dollar spent on planting trees delivers almost six dollars in public benefits. Money is literally growing on trees and yet on average U.S. cities are becoming less green. What is needed is a fundamental shift in our collective attitude: from viewing urban trees as a nicety or useful in the gentrification of neighbourhoods, to seeing them as crucial to climate change mitigation and an essential component to urban living in every neighbourhood. Trees were important before, but they are vital in our climate-altered future.

Madrid is another leading example of a city where citizens are integrating nature into the concrete jungle. The city has always been hot in the summer and it is getting hotter. Temperatures soared to a new high of over forty degrees Celsius during the heatwave in 2017. By 2050, it is projected that Madrid will experience twenty percent more exceptionally hot days, twenty percent less rain, and more deluges of surface water during storms. So what are residents doing in view of more extreme temperature days, more severe droughts, and heavier floods? Madrileños are taking their future very seriously, and covering their city in plants.

The city has expanded existing parks and as many roofs and walls as possible will be covered with greenery. Twenty-two empty lots are being turned into urban gardens with the support of residents. Local companies are coating their buildings with greenery, supported by tax breaks from the city government. At the CaixaForum arts foundation, the giant vertical garden with more than fifteen thousand plants stretches the length of a city block and is as much of an attraction as the exhibits inside the building. Though drought will be more common, the city can water all its plants by redesigning paved areas to capture and store water instead of letting rain run off and go to waste. The smart choice of resilient plants that cope in the arid climate reflects Madrid's reliance on their help rather than on the way they look. In the words of one senior project manager:

Green areas should not be idealised as 'green' themselves. The solutions may look brown at some times of the year, same as the surrounding natural areas. The point is to go with nature's patterns and solutions, not forcing them in any manner for the purpose of achieving a certain look.

The changes that locals in Madrid are making can be adapted to the specifics of any city and its local climate, as many of the effective, low-tech initiatives are universal in principle. Such nature-based solutions have proven co-benefits for our health, economy and the environment. As city dwellers, we need to turn our thinking upside down and turn towards nature instead of away from it. We should rely on what is already around us, and focus our efforts on planting and replanting. Our ingenuity can be employed in revolutionary ways to integrate ecosystems into the cityscape so that our cities are more liveable and resilient. We should stand up to regressive plans to pave over greenery, to grow fewer urban trees, to restrict green roofs and façades. Embedding nature is a strategy for the sustenance of urban life. We need to plant our feet and take a stronger stance.

INITIATIVE

Our footprint is fifty percent too big. Each year we consume around fifty percent more resources than Earth can regenerate. We can look at this footprint locally, and see how much we are contributing to this daunting deficit by measuring our city's over-demand on its ecosystems. On the demand side, a city's ecological footprint accounts for the collective consumption of plant-based food and fibre products, livestock and fish, timber and other forest products, and the space for urban infrastructure and development. At a more personal level, it is the foodstuffs that are grown, processed and transported for us to eat, and all the foodstuffs and packaging that we throw away. It is the water that we use for drinking, cooking and washing, as well as the water that we pour away and flush down the drain. It is the heating and the air-conditioning that we run when we're here and when we're not. It is all the gadgets we accumulate that need electricity whether they are in use or simply waiting to be used. It is the new items that we keep buying but do not keep.

On the supply side, a city's biocapacity represents its biologically productive land and sea areas, including the land used for growing food, fishing waters, and wooded areas to absorb its carbon dioxide emissions from fossil fuels. A city's footprint is the gap between its ecological footprint and its biocapacity, and is an indication of balance or breakdown. We would like to reduce our city's footprint, not out of austerity but out of love of the things we wish to protect. We lead with our convictions by conserving our consumption and by regenerating our supplies. And by doing so, we find our true place.

CONSERVING ENERGY

Energy obesity is pandemic. Many industrial processes require significant amounts of heat and mechanical power, most of which is delivered as electricity or by burning oil and gas. The services sector uses large quantities of energy for lighting and heating, ventilation and air conditioning. At home we consume energy for heating and cooling, lighting and cooking, and to power all sorts of appliances and electronics. It is everyplace. As a result, the potential for saving energy is everywhere and nowhere at the same time. The sheer pervasiveness of opportunities is itself a challenge, as there is no single focal point for us to rally around. Yet it is a pandemic that we cannot allow to continue.

Efficiency gains will have to account for forty percent of the emissions reductions if warming is to be limited to less than two degrees Celsius. Being economical with our energy – using less, or doing more with less – is one of the most constructive and cost-effective ways of mitigating climate change, reducing city air pollution and boosting energy security. It is also one of the quickest actions we can take to turn things around.

Collective action at the local level can add up, as statistics on national energy usage shows. Take the results from the American Council for an Energy-Efficient Economy, an organisation that quantifies energy efficiencies for the world's largest energy-consuming economies. The average score of fifty-one percent indicates the substantial opportunities that exist to save energy wherever you look. Even Germany, with the highest score of seventy-three percent, can still do more. At first glance the surprise in the rankings is the USA, ranked in the top ten despite the absence of national energy conservation plans or binding energy savings goals. Instead, the initiative of U.S. states, cities and citizens is filling this gap in leadership, by implementing more stringent building codes, retrofitting improvements and using smart meters. The groundswell of concern and concerted efforts is yielding a big result.

"Cities that lead on climate, lead on buildings," said New York City Mayor Bill de Blasio when he announced sweeping energy efficiency measures that will reduce the greenhouse gas emissions from the city's over one million buildings. Buildings account for nearly three-quarters of all greenhouse gas emissions in New York City, and since 2014 a ten-year retrofit plan is underway to cut all emissions by eighty percent by 2050 compared to 2005 levels. It is an initiative that resonates strongly with many New Yorkers who live and breathe city life. In the words of one passionate resident:

The list of why I love being a New Yorker can go on and on – no joke. Yet what really makes me proud to call myself a native New Yorker is our mentality. What I am referring to is how environmentally conscious and responsible we are of our actions.

There are many different ways that we can reduce our personal energy consumption, from the mundane to the state of the art. Some changes like resetting the average temperature of heating systems and turning off lights bring energy and cost reductions almost for free and are ridiculously easy to do. Other measures pay for themselves within a short period and then generate healthy returns. If energy efficiencies save us money, why are we not doing it? The real issue is that saving energy is about a change of habit, not about saving small change. When something is preventative (saving energy) as opposed to new (switching to renewables), the benefits may not be as clear to us, and the gains sometimes take longer to accrue. We need help in overcoming these obstacles, more support on the motivation behind not consuming energy.

What does this help look like? Professor Elizabeth Shove of Lancaster University has researched in depth the relationship between individuals' energy consumption, everyday practices and ordinary technology. How people consume energy is influenced by many factors that include belief systems and cultural traits as well as their economic situation, new technology and the prevailing energy infrastructure. Professor Shove calls for the focus to be placed on changing our collective energy consumption practices instead of individual consumer behaviour. The onus is still on us, but social norms tend to lock in our energy usage. By transforming these broader norms through interventions and structural reforms, we are more willing to change our own consumption patterns and become more energy wise.

A technical report by the European Environmental Agency identified the most effective interventions, based on empirical evidence from pilot projects across Europe. The best help in changing personal consumption habits and achieving energy savings is a combination of direct and indirect feedback from energy suppliers. Direct feedback on usage can be given on demand, with information delivered by direct displays, smart meters or prepayment meters. Indirect feedback comes from reflection on usage, for example by making comparisons in billing statements of personal usage against an average or historical trend. In reflecting, target setting to achieve efficiencies can be very effective, especially when we set our own targets.

Help also comes in the form of so-called "inadvertent feedback" when new energy-using equipment is installed. People are naturally interested in how these innovations affect them and become more aware of their energy use, inadvertently reinforcing the changes they wish to make. Community-based initiatives to save energy can also lead to new social norms, and are most successful when group members know each other or are part of a wider programme to reduce their footprint.

Energy efficiency reduces the infrastructure needed for more reserve capacity and fluctuating generating capacity. For legacy cities, the alternative to more efficient usage is to reinforce the existing electricity grid, requiring a much bigger investment given the daunting scale of existing infrastructure. For rapidly growing leapfrog cities in particular, designing urban infrastructure to be less power hungry from the outset is an immediate opportunity to reduce carbon emissions as well as to build cities with lower running costs.

The good news is that it is not too late to avoid the "carbon lock-in" from inefficient, hastily constructed infrastructure. According to the authors of *Equinox Blueprint Energy 2030*, a technological roadmap for a low-carbon future:

Fortunately, the coming expansion of cities provides an unparalleled opportunity – since they have yet to be built – to address a number of social and environmental problems, including the amount of greenhouse gas emissions. Improvements in how urbanisation unfolds are easier to manage, and can have a significant positive impact on energy use and consumption.

If leapfrog cities avoid the typical, high-carbon pathways of legacy cities during their development, they avoid entirely the additional costs of using energy inefficiently and then spending more to upgrade inefficient energy systems. The International Energy Agency found that if cheap, less efficient technologies are chosen in the near term instead of low-carbon alternatives that exist today, the investment cost subsequently needed to meet carbon emissions reductions in power, buildings, industry and transport sectors will quadruple. Where is the sense in stepping over a dollar to pick up a dime?

The energy infrastructure of our city plays an active role in what we consider to be a "normal way of life" and such structural factors as the state of the energy market, energy mix and tariffs determine if some of the ways we can change our usage are even possible. For example, a more liberalised retail energy market provides greater opportunity for us to switch between suppliers, whereas our country's current energy mix limits the immediate choices. Empowerment and taking control of our energy as discussed earlier has a big impact on our ability and motivation to save energy.

We know that saving energy is less expensive than producing energy. It is also a low-cost approach to mitigate greenhouse gas emissions. Making buildings and appliances more energy efficient can be the norm. So too can using them more efficiently. Every one of us can take the initiative simply by making one improvement immediately.

CONSERVING WATER

The importance of clean air and fresh water is revealed by their absence. Cape Town became the first major city in modern times to face the threat of running out of drinking water. "Day Zero" was forecast in April 2018 when dam levels were predicted to be so low that the city government would cease supplying water to households and send people to communal water collection points. Literally, the taps would be turned off.

Cape Town is just one extreme example of the widespread issue of water scarcity facing cities on every continent. An international team of researchers from nine institutions surveyed and mapped the water sources of more than five hundred cities in 2014. They estimated that one in four are in a situation of "water stress". Back then, Cape Town was one of those cities under water stress; four years later its municipal water supply had gone from stressed to dried up. Tokyo, Delhi, Mexico City, Shanghai, Beijing, Kolkata, Karachi, Los

Angeles, Rio de Janeiro and Moscow were identified as the ten largest cities under water stress. A BBC report in 2018 added Sao Paulo, Bangalore, Cairo, Jakarta, Istanbul, London and Miami to this thirsty list.

Underground aquifers have long served as a backup for freshwater in times of drought, storing around thirty percent of the planet's entire freshwater. Dry regions are getting drier and so we are relying increasingly on this groundwater. In addition to drought, inefficient extraction and leaks from ageing municipal water systems, urban population growth and energy consumption all increase our demand for pumping more groundwater. As a damning indictment of our current priorities, however, more is known about oil reserves than underground water reserves.

In 2015, a study led by Tom Gleeson at the University of Victoria in British Columbia concluded that only six percent of the groundwater contained less than two kilometres below the Earth's landmass is renewable within a human lifetime. We are depleting water basins faster than they can recover, with the result that nearly two billion people rely on groundwater that is now considered under threat.

The water shortage in Cape Town gives us all cause to rethink and act differently. After years of trying to get them to conserve more water, residents were shocked into action by the dire announcement of a cut-off date when the city water would run out. Although the instinct was to panic and stockpile more water, millions of Capetonians found ways to curb their usage and reduce water consumption to previously unthinkable low levels. Locals limited themselves to short showers, flushed the toilets less, recycled washing machine water. They stopped washing cars, no longer filled up swimming pools or used drinkable water for gardens. Households that still exceeded strict limits on volume of water faced fines or had a meter installed that would automatically shut off their water. The importance of conserving water was top of mind wherever you went. Everyone was in the same boat and the boat had run onto dry land.

Australians can teach the rest of the world a lot about surviving drought. From 1997 to 2009, the country faced the worst drought in its recorded history. In Melbourne, water levels dropped to an all-time low capacity of twenty-five percent before the drought eased. City residents responded to the escalating crisis by reducing their water demand by almost fifty percent per person, and the actions taken by Melburnians are still used as a roadmap for what residents can do in other water-stressed cities around the world.

The citizens of Cape Town collectively achieved what others considered impossible: cutting their water usage by fifty percent and reducing their daily water usage to fifty litres. (For comparison, the average daily water usage in California in 2016 after four years of drought and water restrictions was still over three hundred litres.) The combination of measures in Cape Town appears to have averted the water crisis for now and the city has pushed back its Day Zero date. Elsewhere around the world, citizens will have to figure out how to do more with less water. It is not a race to the bottom but a race to postpone each city's Day Zero.

The depletion of freshwater reserves is a slow-speed crisis, so there is time to modify current behaviour and take action. Unfortunately we cannot perform miracles and turn brine into water. Seawater desalination currently provides around one percent of the world's drinking water, but it is expensive and no major technology breakthroughs are expected over the next few years that would dramatically lower the cost or improve its efficiency. Municipal water providers can do more to improve the supply of water, often significantly, by upgrading their infrastructure and reducing current leakage levels. For our part, we can do more to reduce the growing demand for potable water. One of the biggest changes is to make use of "greywater", the relatively clean waste water from baths, sinks, washing machines, and other kitchen appliances.

It is a vicious cycle. We use drinking water for a host of things other than drinking. Some of this potable water becomes greywater that we pour down the drain after single use, to be thoroughly contaminated by mixing with toilet-based water. Water is then wasted through leakage to the sewage treatment plant that uses more energy to clean water that could have been reused instead of contaminated and lost. We demand more water because we do not recycle our greywater, and more potable water is then wasted on its way back to us.

We do not have to pour away up to half our usable water. A simple recycling system runs the greywater through a filtration system located in our home and sends the water back for any non-potable use, such as flushing toilets or watering plants. Less water is lost in transit to the sewage works that uses less energy to treat less water. Our demand for potable water is reduced significantly, before we even reduce our overall water consumption.

The interdependency between water and energy is such that there is no energy without water, or water without energy. Electricity is needed to extract, distribute and treat water and wastewater, along with thermal energy (mostly diesel) for irrigation pumps and gas in desalination plants. By taking the initiative to recycle more greywater, we reduce the energy needed for water treatment. Conversely, water is essential for power plant operations as well as for the current production of fossil fuels and biofuels. By pursuing low-carbon alternatives, we reduce the water needed for generating electricity: renewables such as wind and solar photovoltaic require very little water.

Another way for us to reduce our demand on mains water is by capturing more rainwater. For some residents, especially those living in informal settlements not connected to the city's water system, such initiative is a necessity. For example, in a rain-heavy megacity like Mexico City that is plagued by water shortages, rainwater-harvesting systems enable residents to source their own water for up to eight months during the rainy season. It is a potential solution for an increasing number of residents in a city facing increasing water shortages as levels continue to drop in aquifers.

The concept of "water neutrality" may be helpful in prompting citizens, cities and corporations to first reduce their water consumption as much as possible and then to offset their essential water needs by investing in water measures such as conservation and wastewater treatment. As a parallel to carbon neutrality it has the same pitfalls as carbon offsetting, although if we learn from our mistakes it can be an instrument for us to become more water wise, reduce our water footprint, and promote more sustainable use of fresh water.

Whatever we do, we ought to be treating water as a precious and scarce resource. We do not have to wait for our taps to run dry. In the words of one Cape Town resident, "The Day Zero campaign made us all think twice about water. We'll never, ever, ever take water for granted again."

CONSERVING LAND

Urban sprawl is probably best described as the antithesis of an ideal city type. Sprawl – the takeover of rural or agricultural land by low-density city development – has been an issue since Jane Jacobs wrote about it in her classic 1961 book, *The Death and Life of Great American Cities*. She criticised sprawl for, amongst other things, its lack of walkable environments, its lack of mixed-use development and its lack of character, and offered alternative solutions for how cities could flourish to become "congenial places for a great range of unofficial plans, ideas and opportunities". Had there been more understanding of climate change impact and our vulnerabilities, Jacobs would probably have addressed how sprawl exacerbates these issues too.

Compact urban form has since emerged as the central paradigm for sustainable cities. The "compact city" model of urban development is based on relatively high residential density with mixed land uses and an efficient public transport system. It has an urban layout that encourages walking and cycling and a design that reduces energy consumption and pollution. The short distances result in less dependency on private cars, less need for the provision of urban infrastructure and less land use. In a nutshell this model of urban development is "compact, connected and coordinated".

As the saying goes, you can lead a horse to water but you cannot make it drink. Urban planners can give people opportunities to lead a more compact city lifestyle and to move around without private vehicles, but cannot force this way of living upon people. Small home living has big benefits, from saving money to living more simply and even bringing family members closer together. But objects like a big property and a luxury car are status symbols that convey wealth and power in the eye of the beholder. Citizens need to be motivated by other aspirations for the compact city model to be aspirational. As we shall explore in the next chapter, discovering richness has little to do with acquiring such objects.

With increasing threats from climate change, some residents living in areas that are exposed to the impact will embrace compact urbanism as a way to protect themselves. The premise of nascent research is that if an urban development is to expand into a region increasingly vulnerable to natural disasters, denser development will be safer than low-density sprawl within that region. Immediately there would be less area to protect. For example, an exposed coastal city of five hundred thousand people at 1,500 people per square kilometre will occupy over three hundred square kilometres, whereas the same urban population at 5,500 people per square kilometre (the density of the French Quarter in New Orleans) would occupy only ninety square kilometres, a considerably smaller area in need of protection. Other benefits could be the potential for taller and sturdier buildings, the proximity of refuge and options for mass transit evacuation. Not to be underestimated, greater social cohesion in more compact urban areas is also a lifesaver in those communities hit hard by extreme weather.

A strict approach to compact city growth is not a universal paradigm for achieving sustainable urban development. In legacy cities the planning goals may be urban containment and increasing density, whereas in rapidly expanding cities in Asia and Africa the goals may be opening up access to safe and serviced land, or in maintaining rather than increasing the level of urban density. The context is different. For some of these rapid-growth cities, the urban density of their sprawl may be relatively high already and thus compact if not contained. At the same time there can be a high degree of informal and unplanned urban development by people locally that is not compliant with a controlled approach of regulations and enforcement. For expanding cities with dense yet informal settlements, the opportunity to save land and other resources looks a little different.

In his research paper, Donald Brown suggests a deliberate hybrid of modern planning and informal settlement by residents could leapfrog a uniform compact city policy with its requirement for substantial institutional governance. He recognises that informal settlements already possess many of the desired characteristics of compact cities, such as high density and mixed land use, suggesting that much can be learned from them:

[Informal settlements] should be seen as a reflection of local knowledge and skills in production and self-regulation, and that questions concerning whether the compact city is a sustainable urban form, and whether it can provide a vision for rapidly urbanising cities, can be answered through the examination of informal development.

One hybrid approach involves "making room" for urban expansion that would be unrealistic to contain, supporting high-density formal and informal citizen-led development by opening up access to land with planned infrastructure and services. Making room would direct urban development away from hazard-prone areas and ecologically sensitive habitats that would otherwise be overtaken. In another approach, residents themselves take the initiative in upgrading informal housing and infrastructure, in partnership with municipal government. It is the locals who have the knowledge and skills in resilient design and development of high-density environments, borne out of their informal building experience. Both types of hybrid development are deliberately organic and shaped by residents, and therein lies their strength.

The principle of compact urbanism can work everywhere, either by design or organically. Either way, it works by the enlightened self-interest of citizens. An end to mindless urban sprawl will reclaim more land for the common good, to be reused for wider community benefit or remain unused and protected. That would be in everyone's interest.

PROTECTING THE COMMONS

If we are to restore biodiversity, we need to protect the elements of our environment held in common and accessible to all, such as air and water, forests and fisheries. These "commons" belong to everyone and to no one; that is their strength and their weakness. They range in scale from the local green space in your city centre to the high oceans and the atmosphere. Our urbanised world depends heavily on common natural resources such as groundwater basins and marine sand, and common ecosystems such as river deltas and fertile soils. These resources are in dire need of better stewardship as the pace of urban development has overtaken their ability to regenerate.

The "tragedy of the commons" is a notion first published by biologist Garrett Hardin in 1968. He argued that any common resource would always be overexploited because the individual gain of each user outweighs the loss to the common good that each suffers as a result of its over-use. According to Hardin, this free-riding problem cannot be avoided because there is no one to stop it. The real tragedy is that his story is still believed, despite being thoroughly debunked by more well-informed scientists.

A true commons consists not only of a common resource that a community shares and over which it has equal rights, but also of a community that organises itself to manage and protect that resource. Traditional commons, such as shared pastures and managed fisheries, work precisely because they are closely regulated by the people who share them. New commons are emerging all the time, such as local energy co-operatives that generate electricity from wind or solar power.

Conserving these commons is an urban imperative because cities draw on many vital ecosystem services that originate well beyond their municipal boundaries. The distal flows and connections between urban centres and non-urban regions can be as widespread as they are intricate. For Londoners, the area of productive land needed to support their consumption habits and dispose of their waste is over 125 times the size of the city – equivalent to the U.K.'s entire productive land surface. For Hongkongers, the area needed is 450 times as big as the land covered by Hong Kong. Given such interconnectedness, the motivation for conservation by city dwellers is about immediate self-interest as much as longer-term regeneration.

Conventional approaches to managing commons involve either centralised governmental regulation or privatisation of the resource. However, according to political scientist Elinor Ostrom, there is an alternative to the rigid dichotomy between state intervention and the *laissez-faire* workings of the free market. The innovative approach is to set up durable, cooperative institutions that are organised and governed by the resource users themselves. New commons are created by reclaiming the rights over natural resources that belong to no one, and then protecting them with a cooperative community of users. For example, the ocean is arguably not a global commons but a common natural resource in need of "commoning". Depending on the commons, different citizens qualify as resource users and can take the initiative in setting up or participating in such co-ops. Thankfully, Ostrom was concerned with practice as well as theory and delineated eight "design principles" for formalising such self-governing communities.

The Belgian city of Ghent is at the forefront of urban commoning, reconfiguring itself around citizen participation and the sharing of resources. In 2017, city mayor, Termont, commissioned a *Commons Transition Plan* to determine what kind of civic policies should support over five hundred commons-based initiatives that are run by the people of Ghent. These citizen-led commons include Driemasterpark – a park opened on a former industrial site that is entirely managed by nearby residents with a playground, vegetable garden and space for dogs; Urban Agriculture – a working group of individuals and organisations supporting more organic and local food production; Energent – a community-owned, renewable energy cooperative; and co-housing projects, where residents share amenities such as kitchens, guestrooms and laundry rooms. The civic plan represents an ambitious vision of transitioning from "the commons in the city" to "the city as a commons". It also looks beyond Ghent with a view to "translocal" cooperation between cities that would support urban commoning on an even bigger scale.

Urban commons and their emerging economies hold great potential for the social and economic life of a city. They can also play an essential part in an ecological transition, as shared and mutual infrastructures have a dramatically lower city footprint. In an interview, mayor Termont emphasised the connection he sees between participation and future prosperity:

As a city of people, Ghent is firmly convinced that citizens' participation is necessary to successfully deal with today's and tomorrow's city challenges and to retain the prosperity and wellbeing of all residents. Therefore Ghent strongly supports bottom-up initiatives throughout the city. For example, citizens are encouraged to be co-responsible and co-owner of city renewal projects.

Participating in a functioning commons – both urban and natural resource commons – is a powerful part of being a citizen. A commons makes sense of communities as the beneficiaries and the guardians of the common resource. It embeds people both in their natural environment and in the lives of others, and intertwines our urban identity with our ecological identity.

Cities are very dependent on the participation of citizens, on others and on nature, in order to function and to thrive. As residents in our own city we do not live in splendid isolation, lording it over everything else. Perhaps inevitably this myth of our centrality is the last myth to fall. And when it does it is not hard to reimagine the potential for greater wellbeing and enjoyment by being part of something greater than us.

Discovering Richness

PUBLIC AFFLUENCE

Imagine you have whatever objects you need or desire. There is no pursuit to possess something new, no thrill of the chase. You become disinterested in the accumulation of things and possessing them no longer holds any appeal. In such a world people would be free to follow a path that truly defines their place in society, by cultivating their talents and intellects. The essence of such a utopia lies not in the presence of limitless stuff but in the opportunity for each of us to use our talents and intellect to the best of our abilities. With this ultimate goal of human fulfilment in mind we can use our energies to pursue a different kind of affluence, something greater than accumulating and exhibiting wealth.

Affluence has become synonymous with personal wealth in terms of economic wellbeing, although the idea itself is not limited to financial and material accumulation. Personal affluence includes such things as good health, contentment, attachment to others and a sense of belonging. Perhaps it should be no surprise to learn that there is no shortage of the Earth's carrying capacity if we aspire to aggregate human fulfilment over cumulative private consumption. In the bigger context of our rapidly urbanising human population, urban writer Mike Davis goes on to add:

There are innumerable examples and they all point toward a single unifying principle: namely, that the cornerstone of the low-carbon city, far more than any particular green design or technology, is the priority given to public affluence over private wealth... Public affluence – represented by great urban parks, free museums, libraries and infinite possibilities for human interaction – represents an alternative route to a rich standard of life based on Earth-friendly sociality.

This glimpse of a different kind of civic renewal where human energy ebbs and flows freely reveals a way for many more people to attain affluence. Within our grasp is the enjoyment of living affordably together in cities, through access to a wealth of public assets and by actively participating in the life of the city. Public affluence is understood to be as much a collective state of mind as it is the physical places where people congregate and interact. This aspiration is not aligned to any particular political ideology. It is too important locally for national parties to commandeer, and too broad for their tribal partisanship. Far from undermining individualism, it is individual residents and individual cities that will lead this shift towards a broader affluence.

The third imperative of civic revolution is to strive for more social equity as the key to elemental transformation. This key unlocks the potential energy of people, needed in abundance to tackle the people-powered imperative of creating an economy that is restorative and the people-led imperative of protecting biodiversity. How else could meaningful progress be achieved?

Such a renaissance means addressing issues on both sides of the equation: citizens' disengagement and institutional inertia. It requires community involvement and public deliberation, personal commitment and civic reform. More civic energy is needed to propagate city affluence, and it can take many different forms given people's contrasting values and the ways in which our diverse societies are organised. This civic engagement is a balance between rights and responsibilities, a relationship among citizens as well as between citizens and institutions, a spectrum from deliberation to action. It may be tied to democracy or can occur in other political contexts.

Despite its amorphous shape, the essence of civic energy is a set of collective attitudes towards the communal life of the city and actions that improve overall wellbeing. We can advance this agenda with the help of our local politicians, as the decisions made by policy makers are shaped by public opinion and shifting behaviour among residents. By rediscovering our civic voice, we strengthen the social and political bonds within our local communities that are the lifeblood of this broader affluence.

The need for us to belong to a tribe is ingrained and hardwired in our DNA, something that was and still is essential for everyone's survival and wellbeing. Millions of years of evolution have designed us to live and think as community members. However, these age-old social bonds have been weakened over generations by the cumulative impact of industrial revolutions, entrenchment of nation states and pervasiveness of market economies.

In their place new communities have been created to fill the void: the "nation" as the imagined community of the state, the "profession" and "consumer group" as imagined communities of industry and the market economy. They are imaginary because members of a nation state, or people in the same profession, or individuals of a target consumer group, do not know one another in the same way as neighbours in real communities used to know each other. And yet these more imaginary communities have immense power over our thinking today: our attitude of nationalism, fatalism with public life, perspective on work and outlook as consumers. They have a strong hold over us and weaken our willingness to be brave and more engaged in civic life.

Can we imagine a nation without nationalism? The ideology of nationhood can be insidious, as loyalty to the nation state is intentionally built up to surpass more local concerns that are deemed parochial. It is true that people tend to rally around their flag in times of crisis, but going too far spills into jingoism. At the same time, the view on any level less than the nation state is belittled as less significant. It is no coincidence that patriotism applies to nation states only and not cities; there is no single word in the English language to express the sentiment of loving your city. It is no coincidence either that parochialism is mocked as backward looking, and irrelevant to the serious business of state; the particulars are undervalued when there is a broader, abstract worldview to contemplate.

However, cities have their own distinctive ethos that reflects the thinking and actions of their residents. Cities, as much as states, are often the places of collective self-determination. In comparison to the size and complexity of the nation state, cities denote the small and the specific. Residents who take pride in their cities, and the social values these places represent, find ways to nurture their own city's particular ways of life. Often those people who have retained their sense of civic duty and pride do not need a strong dose of nationalism to feel good about themselves. The narrative of nationalism should not trump or replace localism, but instead make room for its rise.

Can we imagine public life without being fatalistic? The present disillusionment with many national governments of the day is due in part to a strong feeling that citizens are too disconnected from the decisions taken on their behalf, and the frustration that politics is too partisan or corrupted. Political crises abound and we are tired of it all. From Brexit to Venezuela, from trade wars to the horror of outright wars. The result of this creeping fatalism towards the imagined "nation" community of the state is a growing dichotomy between a minority of active citizens and the majority who have chosen simply to opt out. While similar criticisms may be levelled at city governance, citizens still feel that they can exert an influence over life in their cities.

The ennui with national politics does not inevitably seep into municipal politics unless we lack the imagination to stop it. As nation states cede more of their powers to regional and municipal governments, metropolitan areas are becoming increasingly important centres of power. Civic engagement is about channelling our newfound power locally to breathe new personal life into the public realm.

Can we imagine identifying with our civic life as much as our work life? For many people the question "Where do you work?" has become shorthand for "Who are you?" There is nothing disingenuous or deceitful about asking such a question, since the answer reveals something about the person and the types of people with whom they choose to spend their time. However, it is an indication of the market's dominant influence on our collective imagination that we associate personal identities with professional institutions and organisations. The problem with using work as a principal point of reference for identity is that desirable professional identities become increasingly exclusive within any organisation. While the few at the top might take pride in jobs that attract high social status, the many who are lower down in the professional pyramid have nowhere to go.

In contrast, such problems do not arise in realising a sense of identity and more of your potential from active citizenship. It is not a zero-sum game. Anyone can participate and make a contribution. Building community becomes increasingly inclusive. Civic life is a complementary path that gives people the additional opportunity to embrace their city as a personal identifier as well as play a meaningful role in the lives of others.

Can we imagine being a partner instead of a consumer? The relationship between citizens and civic institutions has become distorted as we have been branded members of different consumer groups by a market-driven economy. It is unhelpful to consider residents by consumer profiles and the municipality as the provider, when the relationship is more akin to a partnership. We have a right to expect not only that our city is safe and well functioning but also that it is increasingly resilient and more sustainable. We have a right to look to our city to take a stronger lead in creating a restorative urban economy, regenerating the natural resources on which we depend, and increasing public affluence. But with this comes responsibilities on our part to engage in the city life around us to make this happen. When civic engagement is less a consumer transaction and more of a shared stage filled by people with similar ambitions, the rewards are far greater than playing a bit part in an imaginary consumer group.

The notion of public affluence may be less appealing than narrow self-enhancement because the benefits appear to be more indirect. Modern research seems to refute this superficial point, with repeated studies indicating that good relationships – with family and within the community – have more impact on our personal happiness than money and wealth. This age-old finding leads to the surprisingly liberating narrative that happiness is much closer to home than many of us may think, and does not have to cost the Earth either.

Public affluence can have a positive impact on our health too, as it plays an integral part in building and maintaining good social relationships. Professor Holt-Lunstad et al. conducted a review across almost 150 research studies to determine the extent to which social relationships influence the risk of mortality. Their conclusion based on this meta-analysis is that social networks have been shown to be as powerful a predictor of mortality as common lifestyle and clinical risks such as smoking, excessive alcohol consumption and high cholesterol. It is not uncommon for people to feel very strongly about not smoking, or drinking less, or trying to eat some foods and not others. In our attempts to lead healthier lives, building good social relationships is an equally important lifestyle choice. How much more energy would we put into our civic life if we realised that it is also an effective way for all of us to stay healthier for longer?

Technology has its role to play. In the right hands, digital technology helps amplify and orchestrate the social life of the city and the cohesiveness of our communities. It is a potent force in reshaping how we live and work together more resourcefully. Ideally technology enables us to be more connected, to live better on less instead of better on more, and to make fewer resources stretch further. It can put citizens in control and enable a distributed capacity for social interaction and reinvention.

One high-profile example of how citizens became energised with the help of social media was the political momentum created by Bernie Sanders' U.S. presidential campaign in 2016. Two of Sanders' campaigners, Becky Bond and Zack Exley, wrote a book about their experiences entitled *Rules for Revolutionaries: How Big Organizing Can Change Everything.* One of their most powerful insights about galvanising others into action is not about how effective you are in using technology for your message, but in the paradox of the message itself. The more you ask of people, the more likely they are to become involved:

Far more people are willing to step up if you ask them to do something big to win something big than… if you asked them to do something small to win something small.

The proximity and intimacy of local politics turns municipal government into an important place for reinvention. When citizens engage in collaborative governance, public affluence expands even faster. Participatory budgeting is one example of this collaboration, whereby local residents allocate a portion of the municipal budget to city programmes of their choice that they believe serve the greatest need. Originally conceived in the Brazilian city of Porto Alegre, the practice has since spread to hundreds of municipalities across the Americas, Asia and Europe. Similar programmes that foster civic innovation and urban creativity are growing. Mexico City is a great example: Laboratorio Para La Ciudad is a platform for the younger generation to share their ideas and energy to improve civic life through much closer collaboration between Capitalinos and city government.

For decades New Urbanists have promoted city solutions based on compact, pedestrian city centres served by low-carbon transit systems. This formula remains one of the best means of revitalising urban cores and reducing a city's carbon emissions. Given the consequences of our rapidly urbanising population, loss of biodiversity and warming planet, the urgent need is to improve this approach for lasting social and economic vitality. Encompassing previous city solutions, the new formula is framed by a restorative economy, regenerating natural resources and increasing public affluence. It is a civic solution that reconciles our desire for prosperity with the concern that it won't last.

No matter the exact formula, social integration will remain the bedrock for building healthy communities, and accessibility will remain a critical component for people to enjoy the ensuing benefits. Civic life is more commonplace when we include more of the people around us. We have more places in common for civic life, when we make them more accessible. Together, inclusion and access generate affluence in cities and in our own minds, making our lives richer.

INCLUSIVENESS

Over two billion more people will be living in cities within the next thirty years, at the same time as we are dealing with the fallout of climate change and loss of biodiversity. In effect we will be doubling today's urban population by 2050, and how each of us chooses to live in these urban settlements will be a major factor in the success or failure of mitigating climate chaos and reducing the rate of extermination.

Cities are fundamentally about people and are a manifestation of the kind of humanity we bring to bear. Much depends on how we shape our cities: our environmental impact, our social wellbeing, our economic vitality, our sense of community and connectedness. The places where people go and where they meet are at the core of what makes a city work. Perhaps more important than the buildings in a city, it is the public spaces in between that make people and place come together.

Most urban planners are familiar with Nolli maps, first devised by Italian architect Giovanni Nolli in the eighteenth century. His radical approach to urban development was essentially about planning the spaces before the buildings. He started with the public realm, then considered the best layout of streets and squares, and finally decided where the buildings should be located. Nolli is best known for his map of Rome in which buildings and space are inverted – space is marked black and buildings are left white. This reductionist plan omits almost all levels of information – contours, urban infrastructure, administrative boundaries, landscape features, street names – to show just the plan form of buildings. In depicting only the footprints of buildings, the plan emphasises the voids formed by streets, squares and outdoor areas, revealing the accessibility and flow of space within a city. These figure-ground graphics of urban layouts have become very popular today, rivalling skyline silhouettes and the images of iconic buildings. Their ability to evoke a city's uniqueness reveals much about the importance and appeal of un-built public spaces in our urban landscape.

The public realm has two roles: it embodies the common good and is the dwelling place of our civic life and our civilisation. It takes many different forms, from market squares and plazas to pedestrian streets and parklets. These public spaces are the connective tissue of urban life and have a profound impact on the character of communal activity and the enactments of public life. The public realm helps us navigate not only geographically but also culturally – where we have come from, what we value, where we are going.

Public spaces have power. They influence the people that use them and to a much wider degree the number of people who feel a stronger attachment to their city simply by knowing that they are there. Every city has its unique combination of these public spaces that captures the minds and affections of its residents. Place de la République in Paris, Central Park in New York City, Sambodromo stadium in Rio de Janeiro, Long Street in Cape Town – the list goes on. It is also a very personal list: we may live in the same city but the public spaces that are close to my heart will be different from the ones close to yours.

It is the "spaces in between" that give great cities and neighbourhoods their distinctiveness by enabling people to congregate and interact. When we're in Paris or New York, we know we're in Paris or New York. Within those cities, if we are in the Marais district of Paris or Tribeca in New York, the character and public spaces of those neighbourhoods remind us of where we are. Public spaces are powerful enough to change how you feel about your city, how you live in your city, how involved you are in your city.

Despite their wide variety, vibrant public spaces share three simple characteristics. Firstly, they are well defined, so we know clearly when we have arrived. Secondly, they are emphatically public, open and accessible to the wonderful complexity of city life around them. Thirdly, they come to life through our humanity, rather than by a master plan, shining when people fill them and they reflect the spirit of the city.

It is not uncommon to feel lonely in a big city. We do not make new social connections simply by living close to lots of other people. Instead, these connections are encouraged by the presence of the public spaces that attract a mix of people and invite them to dwell. London, for example, has almost fifty large parks and open commons, many hundreds of smaller public places, and over thirty thousand allotments where residents can grow their own fruit and vegetables. These kinds of places are some of the most socially powerful spaces in the city because they are open to residents and not hidden behind closed doors. The point of public spaces is not to be attractions for us to come and look at, but to create communal places where people attract other people. Benches, gardens, water fountains, outdoor exercise gyms and play parks can all provide this focus. It is the thoughtfulness of these smaller signs of community and their humanity that makes people feel attached to their city.

The Ancient Greeks and Romans believed their city-states should provide dramatic spaces as a source of civic pride and a spectacular backdrop for the daily life of citizens. The inspiring public forums in Athens and Rome are examples of this "scene painting". Fast-forward two thousand years and scenography still plays its part in place making. The *London Plan* – the overall spacial development plan for London –

has policies specific to city views and vistas that "contribute towards making London a special place and improve quality of life". There are three types of strategic views designated in the *London Plan*: London panoramas, river prospects and townscapes. These views are seen from places that are publicly accessible and well used; include significant buildings or urban landscapes that help to define London; and are protected from new property developments that may interfere and hence diminish the designated public realm backdrop. Although judgments as to what may harm or enhance this scene painting are subjective, the principle and civic debate are as important as the outcome.

The enduring value of great public spaces is the continual occurrence of events by chance, to the benefit of those who are there and the wider population. This social development in city life happens naturally when diverse, cohesive communities are living in a vibrant urban space. However, this does not occur without deliberate effort and energy in creating and protecting such public spaces, as there is always a tension between differing claims on this space from commercial interests and from those interested in the common good of the city. These two goals are often not aligned, as Amanda Burden, New York City's chief city planner under the Bloomberg administration, elaborates:

Commercial interests will always battle against public space. It might mean more money for the city, but a city has to take the long view: the view for the common good. No matter how popular and successful a public space may be, it can never be taken for granted. Public spaces always need vigilant champions, not only to claim them at the outset for public use, but to design them for the people that use them, then to maintain them to ensure that they are for everyone, that they are not invaded, abandoned or ignored.

Despite the rapid urban expansion over the next few decades, building neighbourhood communities and a sense of collective identity takes time. Even cities that are efficient and function well (in terms of their transportation systems or utilities, for example) can be desolate habitats for people if they do not support a thriving social life. A sociable city creates networks of these public spaces large and small, accessible without private transport; citizens create the richness by filling them and looking after them. In such urban environments we are never far from a social oasis or a place where we may pick up new habits from one another. These cities are quicker to evolve and adapt, as there is less entrenched resistance by residents to change and new norms of behaviour spread more readily.

Place making works by virtue of the different people who live locally and interact, and falls short when those same people move away because they cannot afford to live locally. The social fabric must be underpinned by a mix of housing in each neighbourhood and by increased housing stock where there are shortages. Does any dynamic or fast-growing city not have a housing shortage or insufficient choice? It is fundamental to the amenity and liveability of an area that there is diversity in the locations, types and prices of housing to match the diversity of people who would like to live there. It is the mix of people that adds richness and makes a place real.

On the one hand a decrease in housing affordability is indicative of the economic success of a neighbourhood. On the other hand it erodes the social benefits of place making and ultimately threatens future levels of productivity. When rents and house prices rise beyond the reach of average working families, a host of key workers within the local community from teachers to police officers and nurses are forced to move out. This impacts not only the local economy but also the multifaceted make-up of the neighbourhood.

The importance of social diversity to public affluence is not lost in the *London Plan*. Although almost five hundred pages, the entire plan can perhaps be summarised in three lines: maintain urban growth within the Green Belt boundary; identify development opportunity areas that can absorb this future growth; allow development only if it is mixed-use, includes affordable housing and has good access to public transport. Reading between these lines the message is clear: cosmopolitan London will not survive if it becomes a city of enclaves.

To avoid the social consequences of segregation, cities need to invest in more socially intelligent systems for housing. For example, monolithic public housing developments should give way to pepper-pot distribution of rent-subsidised apartments within mixed buildings; affordable housing that may include accommodation for the elderly, disabled or students should not be distinguishable from the outside. Citizens can also take the lead by setting up housing co-operatives or running community self-build projects. Equally, we can avoid voluntary segregation from the rest of society and not cut ourselves off from one another by retreating into gated developments. A "gated community" is an oxymoron: research indicates that most people who live on gated streets do not want to get involved with their neighbours or local community.

The secret ingredient to public affluence is more balanced communities, not divisiveness. To stay ahead of their own growth, leapfrog cities need to find effective ways to integrate their burgeoning informal settlements. Disparagingly labelled as slums, ghettos or shanty towns, these informal settlements can be home to significant numbers of city residents and represent a vital pool of local labour. These citizens already live in far more compact and resourceful ways than residents elsewhere. Segregated, they cleave the city and their neighbourhoods become places where inequalities and poverty are exaggerated.

This outcome is by no means inevitable as citizens can integrate more easily if their areas are woven into the fabric of the city to avoid such polarisation. Accessibility can be improved by extending public transport services and by thinking innovatively of connections that suit the terrain, such as cable cars that link up hillside neighbourhoods. Place making by citizens can be encouraged with the support of municipal government, for instance by investing in attractive public buildings that are sited in these areas or by establishing property ownership rights for residents of informal settlements. Citizen-led approaches to more hybrid development schemes keep in touch with our humanity, and avoid the brutal diktat of clearing settlements only to replace people's former homes with ill-suited, cookie-cutter building schemes.

Diversity of local residents may be the key that unlocks the power and potential of public affluence, but its importance to society is even broader. There is a direct link between this social cohesiveness and sustainable development. If new cities follow the well-worn approach to urban development, the pressure will be on constructing buildings with little regard or budget for the public realm. In the worst case, housing enclaves will be constructed to perpetuate separation, with gated communities here and tower blocks there. The priority will simply be "roofs over heads" as if there were a forced choice between planning new buildings and planning diverse social spaces in between. As Nolli demonstrated, inverting this thinking by putting the public realm first is a leapfrog opportunity that encourages a more inclusive society by giving citizens space for sociality. It is even more important that the most rapidly growing cities, with the least time for communities to develop, allow for these social spaces that strengthen the nascent bonds within and between communities.

Great public places are great because people use them creatively and in doing so create affluence in its broader and more appealing sense. We become attached to them and to others who share these same spaces with us. The opportunity cost of people feeling separated and disconnected is measured by the lack of community spirit and ailing civil society. There is no sustainability without diverse and inclusive places in our cities for us to share our finite resources more humanely while also nourishing the human spirit. They are part of the collective genius of city life. As citizens, we make the difference by making the places come alive.

AUDACITY

If cities belong to people, why are we building them for cars? Before the advent of the automobile, city streets were human spaces. They were thoroughfares and also public places where people would meet, socialise and sell goods. Everyone was included when automobiles were excluded. Today the common perception is that our streets are the exclusive domains of motorised vehicles, and with this takeover the focus instead is on improving road safety and reducing traffic pollution.

If this is the priority then there is clearly more work to be done on both counts. In Europe and the USA, over one hundred thousand people are killed in road accidents every year. Globally, that figure is over one million, with an additional twenty to fifty million injured or disabled. At the same time the transport sector as a whole is responsible for almost one quarter of the entire energy-related greenhouse gas emissions globally, and its emissions are increasing at a faster rate than any other sector. Vehicles with petrol and diesel engines also produce fine particulate matter and toxic nitrogen oxides, a fact that has come into even sharper focus in the wake of the VW scandal in 2015 and their exhaust emissions cover-up.

The automobile is not the most efficient form of urban transportation. Far from it, as a recent European report from the Ellen MacArthur Foundation points out with an array of dismaying facts:

The European car is parked ninety-two percent of the time – often on valuable inner-city land. When the car is used, only one-and-a-half of its five seats are occupied. Less than twenty percent of the total petroleum energy is translated into kinetic energy, and only one thirteenth of that energy is used to transport people. As much as fifty percent of inner-city land is devoted to mobility (roads and parking spaces). But, even at rush hour, cars cover only ten percent of the average European road. Yet, congestion cost approaches two percent of GDP in cities like Stuttgart and Paris.

Auto manufacturers are keen to promote more fuel-efficient engines today, more electric cars tomorrow and more autonomous vehicles in the future, as the solution to an urban challenge that is more complex and diverse than driving. It is no surprise that this is their view of the world, as they see everything from the vantage point of the driver's seat of a car. As Abraham Maslow said, "I suppose it is tempting, if the only tool you have is a hammer, to treat everything as if it were a nail." It is all too easy to lose our perspective in all the high-octane-fuelled advertising and in the fantasies of open roads, believing the hype that cars are a status symbol instead of a stasis symbol.

Beyond the zeitgeist of reinventing the automobile remains the more human consideration of developing modern cities as habitats for people and not cars. The suitability of automobiles in the evolving urban context is even more questionable as building cities around them increases congestion, encourages urban sprawl and discourages the use of public transport. What would things look like instead if we are daring enough to change our urban traffic culture fundamentally, from catering to the exclusiveness of private automobiles to embracing the inclusiveness of walking, cycling and public transport?

Take London as one example of the massive potential of this mind shift in mobility. Londoners take a staggering total of almost twenty million trips each day. A policy analysis report by Transport for London discovered that of these trips, thirteen million are made by motorised transport and over half of these are short enough that they could potentially be cycled instead. The greatest potential for cycling comes from people travelling by car: for every trip currently made by rail or Underground that could be cycled, there are more than five made by car. The most significant barrier to realising this potential? Most trips that could be cycled would be made by people who currently do not cycle at all. Looking to the future of urban transport, the report concluded with the call to action: "We need to encourage people who don't cycle to start."

China puts a lot of emphasis on technological advancement. In a deliberate analogy to the "four great inventions" of Ancient China – the discovery of papermaking, gunpowder, printing and the compass – the country claims "four new great inventions" of modern times. Although China has not invented any of these four new technologies, it has outpaced other nation states in their widespread implementation and adaption. What are these four new great inventions? E-commerce, mobile payments, high-speed rail and bike sharing. Chinese firms like Mobike and Ofo lead dock-less bike sharing, where users locate bikes with their smartphone and leave them anywhere without having to park them at a specific dock. Big spending by these two rival companies colonised cities with their bikes. It has not been a completely smooth ride, with oversupply of new bikes clogging city streets, and theft and vandalism by users. Nonetheless, the vice minister of China's Ministry of Transport estimated that there were four hundred million registered bike-sharing users in 2018 and twenty three million shared bikes. In short, rapid advancement in mass active transport across hundreds of cities, as China proudly embraces its title as the "kingdom of bicycles".

The exemplar of the future of active transport in urban areas is Copenhagen. There are more bikes than inhabitants in a city where less than thirty percent of households own a car. There are over four hundred kilometres of designated cycle lanes in the city. When asked, only one percent of Copenhageners who cycle mention environmental issues as the main reason: cycling is the preferred means of transport because it is the quickest and easiest way to get around town. A well-designed bicycle infrastructure that gives preference to riders instead of drivers entices people to overcome their prejudices and use it, and creates a virtuous cycle. As bicycle traffic increases, car traffic reduces, encouraging more people who do not cycle to start.

Rush hour in Copenhagen is made up of several hundred thousand people riding their bikes to work on lanes that favour cyclists. "Green Wave" routes on Nørrebrogade and other major arteries in the city coordinate the traffic lights for cyclists, so if they ride at a speed of twenty kilometres per hour they will hit green lights all the way into the city in the morning rush hour. The wave is reversed in the afternoon so bicycle users can ride home non-stop, avoiding the tailbacks enjoyed by motorists. As bike culture spreads, so do cycle lanes. Cycle super highways lead cyclists in and out of Copenhagen from as far away as fifteen kilometres (a distance that Transport for London considered to be well beyond the maximum distance that would realistically be cycled).

Rotterdam, the second largest city in the Netherlands, is experimenting with heat sensor operated traffic lights for cyclists. The lights can sense the number of cyclists waiting at the red light. During rush hour, when there is a group of about ten cyclists the light will turn green longer and more often so they can continue in a steady flow while cars wait. The city is also trialling rain sensors that make the lights go green more frequently for cyclists when it is raining.

Active transport includes walking as well as cycling. Beyond Europe and North America, cities that have a high proportion of pedestrian traffic can reinvent mobility by focusing on pedestrians as an asset, leapfrogging the North American model that requires long commutes in private vehicles to work. For example, in India, one-third of residents in megacities who have to travel to work go by foot and ten percent cycle. In terms of the number of residents who use active transport, these cities are ahead of their time and not behind.

Walkability depends on a number of factors including urban connectivity, safety and pedestrian infrastructure. Walkers are hindered in cities like Delhi by footpaths that are dilapidated and overgrown; blocked by parked cars or occupied by street hawkers; cluttered with rubbish or strewn with electric wires. Unfortunately it is all too easy for city streets to become unfriendly for pedestrians and bicycles, as an oversight of rapid urbanisation. Public space along the side of roads is squeezed or simply taken over by motorbikes. Cities like these often overlook walkers and cyclists, failing to capitalise on the inherent advantages of people using active transport.

What if traffic engineers in leapfrog cities (and elsewhere for that matter) were bold enough to reallocate road space based on equity of use, instead of widening roads and building more flyovers to try to ease congestion for the minority of private vehicle users? Different modes of transport would be assigned space based on the number of people who benefit, promoting more effective mass transit and creating a cleaner environment with more walkers and cyclists. Making these cities pedestrian and cycle-friendly would drastically improve urban mobility and also make them more inclusive by encouraging all residents to think differently about how they move around. Such a leap in development takes not only imagination but also the courage to act on the scale that is needed.

Different stakeholders, from auto manufacturers to technology companies, herald autonomous vehicles as the future of mobility. However, driverless vehicles are not so much a panacea that will give us independence from driving as a Pandora's Box of foreseen and unforeseen consequences. Driverless vehicles may be liberating, freeing people's time to do other things while travelling and offering independence to people who cannot drive. They promise safe, fast and congestion-free transportation – just as the first automobiles did before them. They also bring technical hurdles, a new layer of complexity to urban planning and safety, and could increase congestion by making road travel easier for people or simply by filling up the streets with automated delivery vehicles.

One of the less obvious but more profound shifts in a future with driverless vehicles is the potential blurring with public transport. According to David Lesne of UBS, once the car becomes autonomous the relevance of car ownership drops materially. Hence the real focus of mobility in cities beyond active transport is not on futuristic cars but more broadly on passenger services, on the art of sharing rides and the science of filling seats. The principle for determining where autonomous vehicles belong in the urban landscape should be based on the context of the wider transport system. For example, they could be integrated to fill gaps in public transport and cover the "last mile" to ferry people from stations to their neighbourhoods. Alternatively, they could be used as a primary means of transport with a designated lane and reduce urban living space wasted on parking.

In rapidly growing cities, urbanisation continues to outpace the innovation in transportation. Yet if the example of autonomous vehicles in urban areas is ultimately nothing more than a new way of making public transport more viable, leapfrog cities can take a less complicated and more affordable route into the future. For example, the Delhi municipal government is expanding its Bus Rapid Transit System with vehicles powered by compressed natural gas that greatly reduce emissions as well as with new electric buses. Routes are being revised to avoid overlapping, integrate better with the metro network, and cover as many areas as possible with more effective outreach. A planned thirteen-kilometre express bus service corridor would also avoid congestion along a dedicated new route from Karawal Nagar in the northeast of the city and Mori Gate bus terminal, improving passenger services while reducing the need for so many private vehicles.

The revolution in urban mobility will depend not on a technology, but on whether we change our attitudes and adapt to various forms of transport that are more appropriate for city living. The world-class Delhi metro system is a poignant case. The massive network of 252 kilometres of track with 185 stations was completed before time and within budget. Trains are air-conditioned and run on time. It is eco-friendly and became the first metro rail system in the world to claim carbon credits for reducing greenhouse gas emissions by reducing pollution levels in the city by 630,000 tons of carbon dioxide equivalent a year. The metro system serves an average of almost three million passengers a day or over one billion passengers every year. Just what this city and many cities like it need!

By almost any metric the Delhi metro is an exemplary success story. But very few of its riders come from the city's most wealthy classes, who prefer instead to sit in traffic jams inside their private vehicles on congested roads. Some Delhiites have drivers so they can do other things while being driven, although this alleviates a symptom and not the cause.

A local Uber driver sheds light on the social divide: "I go on the metro, I'm a poor person... but why would a rich person go on it, in the middle of all the crowds? They'll hire a car or taxi or take their own car." Too many residents in too many cities regard public transport as something for those who cannot afford to drive. This is backwards thinking. Private vehicles are not suitable for city living, regardless of their affordability. To paraphrase Enrique Peñalosa, mayor of Bogota, what we aspire to is a city not where the poor move about in cars but where the rich take public transport.

Traffic congestion is a social dilemma similar to the Prisoners' Dilemma in game theory. If, for example, we trust each other not to drive private vehicles in city centres and everyone uses active transport on a well-designed public transport system, we each give up our exclusive automobile and are equally rewarded with no gridlock. However, if some defect to their private vehicles while most still use alternative means, those defecting will benefit more from traffic-free roads and the convenience of their own personal transport. When everyone sees the benefits enjoyed by a few drivers and defect *en masse*, then the outcome is gridlock and everyone loses. In too many places where there is not enough trust or where segments of society are unwilling to share similar modes of transport, we see gridlock. When we live in proximity to one another, attempting to move around in a way that excludes others is the least convenient option for everyone.

In addition to less congestion and more urban space for living and sociality, there is another universal benefit in shunning private vehicles with combustion engines: less choking air pollution. From particulate matter to ground-level ozone to sulphur dioxide, nitrogen dioxide and carbon monoxide, air pollution in all its different forms affects everyone. It is one of the most critical health threats in many cities, causing hundreds of thousands of premature deaths a year.

The most recent air quality data released by the World Health Organisation (covering over four thousand towns and cities in over one hundred countries) revealed that over half of the total urban population worldwide lives in cities that exceed recommended levels of airborne pollutants. Outdoor particulate matter in cities comes largely from motorised vehicles, industry and power plants burning fossil fuels. The transition to renewable energy for electricity removes a proportion of the pollution; the remaining irritants are the chugging petrol and diesel vehicles crammed on our streets.

If you have the choice, should you be taking public transport instead of driving? Ask yourself instead if you care enough about traffic congestion and local air pollution to do something about how you choose to move around town. Undeniably your city can do more to alleviate both problems, but the city is not solely responsible. Hanging in the air is also the question, "What more can you do?"

Transport in all its various forms is literally a means to an end. What we are really striving for by living in a city is accessibility. According to Harvard professor of economics Edward Glaeser, cities exist to eliminate transport costs for people, goods and ideas. In hyper-dense Hong Kong, people may have access to everything they need within five minutes and live only fifteen minutes from their workplace. Transport and compact living are inextricably linked.

However, it is very difficult to transition from a car-dependent lifestyle to a dense metro lifestyle once the city's infrastructure has been established. Here lies another opportunity for rapidly developing cities to overtake the legacy model of an urban system designed for the automobile, by focusing on urban form and proximity that dramatically improve accessibility for more people and thereby reducing the need for movement itself.

Accessibility for more people to the richness of city life adds to its richness. Whereas the built environment locks in certain patterns that make movement easy or difficult, our willingness to adopt different ways of moving around makes living in cities either inexorably easier or more difficult for everyone. Forget the car and reclaim city streets for people. Breathe easier. Go with the flow, or else there will be no flow.

Inspiring Revolution

LEADERSHIP

We have reached what some activists are calling "Decade Zero" – the last few years in which we can still tackle dangerous climate change if we take the necessary drastic action. It is a moot point whether we still have time to avoid irreversible climate change. Humanity's lack of inclination to change course and ongoing procrastination about warming temperatures is like the familiar maxim of a frog in hot water: if you put one in boiling water it will hop out, but if you gradually increase the temperature of the water it will let itself be boiled. The proverb warns us about the need to take action against slowly developing dangers, in addition to the immediate ones that are more obvious. The maxim breaks down in real life, for the frog at least; our long-legged friend is smart enough to jump out long before the water gets too warm.

Due to the disparity in the effects of climate change around the world, there may not be a single event that will signal immediate danger and unite action. However, the prospect of disruption is no less real or imminent simply because we are distracted from noticing the signs, or do not have the time or inclination to do something. According to the authors of the *One Degree War Plan*:

Given the physical momentum for change already in the climate system and the continuing lack of action on the scale and with the urgency required, it is now too late to prevent major disruption and damage in the decades ahead, as a result of inaction over the past several decades. We believe there will now be an ecological and economic crisis, of a scale that is significant in the history of human life on earth. But we certainly do not believe it is too late to prevent the collapse of the global economy and civilisation.

"Too late" is not a single date. There is no too late, because action we take today will still reduce the level of future hardship and damage. Our collective response happens locally, and hence the places where citizens take the lead now will be best placed to last.

There are leaders and there are those who lead. If you have already made personal changes for the better, then you are one of those who lead. But it does not stop there because other people need to see someone change first before they choose to follow. They notice the bigger commitments that are not so easy to reverse or so easy to make: the solar panels on your roof; the type of vehicle that you buy or don't buy; the decision to live in a smaller house or to move into an apartment. They notice your commitment of time: to environmental projects; to community action groups that improve liveability; to supporting progressive city officials. People take note when you lead by following your beliefs.

The real effort in building cities that last is in changing human behaviours, and in acting now in the face of seemingly remote danger. It is an issue of habit rather than habitat, as cities embody the interactions of the people who live there. Greensburg's story is one of enduring relationships, when the Kansas town itself was almost entirely destroyed by a tornado over ten years ago. It is also a story of leadership when neighbours rebuilt the town to become one of the greenest in the USA. Work to clear the wreckage of the town started almost immediately after the tornado, with residents holding weekly meetings in tents to discuss their plans. According to mayor Bob Dixson, "The number one topic at those tent meetings was talking about who we are – what are our values?" Looking back today at the remarkable civic renewal he acknowledges, "We learned that the only true green and sustainable things in life are how we treat each other."

The imperatives are the same for all of us, and not unique to those cities that face the most immediate dangers. If we are to prosper in the longer term we need to rebuild a new economy that is based on restorative development; look after ecosystems that support our entire way of life; and strengthen communities as the key to unlocking more potential energy. There is plenty of room to make a profit in a zero-carbon, circular economy, but profit alone is not the motive for this great civic transformation. There is plenty of room to co-exist with nature, but shrinking humanity's footprint is not the rallying cry. There is plenty of room to be more equitable, but that is not the catalyst for our collective preservation. The hope and the goal are for lasting social and economic vitality locally, for civilisation as a whole.

There may be three broad reactions by incumbents resistant to the new narrative, to its aspiration and the call for massive change. Each brings with it a particular notion of expertise and where that expertise resides. The first is the "In the real world..." opposition to challenging the status quo, from people and companies who present themselves as experts by virtue of their everyday success in the current paradigm. The second reaction is the "Breakthrough technology is the real answer" alternative to changing our behaviour from well-intentioned innovators and technology gurus, who are experts because they appear closer to the technicalities. The third dismissal is the "Global solutions for global problems" attitude from people who are not necessarily attached to a particular place, and consider their expertise as seeing the bigger picture. Let's address each one in turn.

In the real world change is a constant. There is a point at which oversized organisations and imagined communities simply become too complex to hold everyone together. Perhaps this point has been reached, which would go some way to explain our multifaceted crisis. Like past revolutions, the result is likely to be a shift of power away from where it is currently concentrated and enjoyed. There is inevitable tension between rising urban power locally on the one hand and the established powers of nation states and multinational corporations on the other. Tethered by independence and competition respectively, these two incumbents may be unable to rise to the challenge of a new world order that is defined increasingly by more local forces that are collaborative and networked.

Many technologists have argued convincingly for the positive impact of breakthrough technology on society and its welfare. However, there is a distinct difference between thinking of technology as an enabler and thoughtless reliance on technology. There is a gulf between what has driven us to exceed planetary boundaries and a belief in eco-technology as the solution to extend these boundaries. Our tendency to expect the ongoing invention of new technologies to overcome our limitations is missing the bigger point, as it removes invention from people's behaviour and diminishes their personal responsibility to change. The argument of breakthrough technology is not the exclusive arena of those with the technical details but is much broader, as it necessarily involves influencing people's opinions and changing their habits.

As for leadership in solving global solutions, no one level of society has a superior view or a monopoly. Citizens have formidable potential energy because cities are the focal points in implementation. As former New York City mayor Mike Bloomberg said, "the difference between my level of government and other levels of government is that action takes place at the city level." They are the places that are the first to experience trends and the first-responders in a crisis. Engaged city residents and independently minded cities can move faster than their sprawling nations, and this is a critical advantage given the urgency of some of the social and environmental challenges we face.

If cities have a future – economic, social and ecological – this future begins with a deeper appreciation of the shared leadership role we must play. Cities that last need not wait for the complexities of inter-national alignments or global agreements to be resolved. Civic leadership, operating locally and cooperating broadly, is vital to renewal on a human scale yet with the potential for global reach.

MEASURING UP

What should count as progress in redressing an unsustainable economy and an unstable environment? It is often said that we cannot manage what we do not measure. However, the true measure of prosperity cannot simply be expressed in one economic indicator, despite our stubborn belief that Gross National Product is such a proxy. In a speech almost half a century ago, U.S. senator Robert Kennedy's words still ring true today on how Gross National Product falls short:

[Our GNP] counts napalm and counts nuclear warheads and armoured cars for the police to fight the riots in our cities... Yet the GNP does not allow for the health of our children, the quality of their education or the joy of their play. It does not include the strength of our marriages, the intelligence of our public debate or the integrity of our public officials. It measures everything in short, except that which makes life worthwhile. And it can tell us everything about America except why we are proud that we are Americans. If this is true here at home, so it is true elsewhere in world.

In contrast, Bhutan's supplementary yardstick to Gross National Product is based on indicators that look beyond economics to an "aggregate final optimal value which we call happiness". Even though their Gross National Happiness index has raised interest internationally, it is difficult to persuade countries to look beyond development conclusions driven by production, expenditure and income. Yet as Dasho Karma Ura, President of the Centre for GNH Research, comments, "Life is not sequential like this. You don't say that I want to become rich first and happy later." What Kennedy did not know, and Ura started as a thought experiment, is that a thriving economy and society that is sustainable can also make people richer and happier. Indicators that are grounded in this reality will measure what makes worthwhile life possible.

The measure of citizens' prosperity should be apparent by looking at a very small number of indicators. Any more and we cannot see the wood for the trees. They should capture our collective urban efforts and be a blend of place and of people, reflecting the grain of the built environment and the civic attitudes of those who live there.

There are local priorities specific to each city that cannot be ignored, as they help maintain a functioning urban society and build its resilience. For example, utilities are essential services and may be a local priority: for one city this could mean the provision of adequate electricity or water supply; for a different city, the provision of universal broadband connectivity. Another local priority may be to improve healthcare for a growing population or social care for an ageing one. Whereas city-specific priorities focus on immediate pressure points, the collective urban efforts that we measure are the stuff of epochal shifts. We need both.

Lasting prosperity encompasses our individual and collective wellbeing as well as that of the environment. How this materialises depends on us, on how much we care about where our energy comes from and how much stuff we waste; whether we reconnect with nature and whether we reconnect nature with our urban environment; if we feel a shared sense of identity and belonging with those around us and if we behave accordingly.

If our future depends on these behaviours, we need indicators that measure our welfare in a different light. Gross Domestic Product has been used as a reference (at various points in this book) primarily because it is common ground with the economic narrative of today and it is the language best understood by business leaders and policymakers. But it is only a bridge to help others relate to what really counts, and no longer the destination. It does not embody the imperatives we face or convey any sense of transformation. Instead, the measure of our future prosperity is framed in terms of human potential ("social capital"), our capacity to thrive ("city biodiversity") and people-led progress ("clean growth").

SOCIAL CAPITAL

The lasting impact of civic engagement is the increase in "social capital" – the bonds and bridges between people with a shared sense of belonging and identity. These are the links and common values we share that enable us to trust one another, building the foundation for better cooperation and innovation. Social capital is essential, as everyone has a role to play if we are to remake our economy and to regenerate the means of securing the necessities of life. Our human potential is boundless, but will not come to fruition without shared aspirations and purpose. United, we stand.

There is no single form of social capital: some forms are formal, such as memberships of organisations, whereas others are very casual like the group of people who gather regularly in one of the neighbourhood cafés. As a consequence of its richness and diversity, social capital is not easy to quantify, yet we need to take its measure because it affects fundamentally our individual wellbeing and collective ability to change.

There are a host of potential measures, any one of which is imperfect. One set of indicators may look at formal memberships and participation in different kinds of informal networks. Another may turn instead to social trust as a close proxy, basing surveys on the simple question, "Do you trust your neighbours?" It is not important to use one particular metric or social capital index – you need to see the trend. Your target is to be the change you want to see. Your city's target is to see an increase in this social capital within each neighbourhood.

CITY BIODIVERSITY

Urban patterns of population growth and economic activity may vary, but all cities rely on biodiversity in order to function and on its embarrassment of riches in order to prosper. Loss of biodiversity has an increasingly serious impact on all our livelihoods and capacity to thrive. Something else has to give. We need to internalise our city's reliance on biodiversity and ecosystem services, and quantify its regeneration as a measure of our capacity to thrive. An objective, scientifically credible metric exists. The *City Biodiversity Index* was formulated by Singapore's National Parks Board, in cooperation with the United Nations and a taskforce of international experts. More than fifty cities around the world are working with this self-assessment tool, tracking their native biodiversity, ecosystem services, and collective stewardship of these natural resources.

The year in which a city embarks on this scoring system is taken as the baseline year and future years are measured against this benchmark to chart progress in conserving biodiversity. The true measure of success is the regular and long-term application of this indicator by cities, and the resulting best practices municipalities adopt to ensure sustainable urban development and citizens adopt to live more sustainably in their surroundings. The target is to evaluate your city's progress, with the collective aspiration of restoring local biodiversity and regenerating irreplaceable ecosystems.

CLEAN GROWTH

Continued progress is possible through "clean growth" that entails powering our cities with endless renewable energy, decoupling growth from material consumption, and eliminating waste and pollution. In other words, striving for a practical utopia based on one hundred percent renewables and a fully circular city. One aggregate measure of this progress is an Emissions Intensity Ratio, defined as the amount of greenhouse gases produced for each unit of Gross Metro Product created. Clean growth does not necessarily require economic expansion, as a stable urban economy could be growing its share of clean energy, or the urban economy could continue to grow by taking a circular route to make resources more productive.

As the name suggests, this indicator is dynamic as we grow by putting these connected pieces in place. The target is to reduce the Emissions Intensity Ratio continuously by lowering emissions and growing the circular economy. National targets were set in the Paris Agreement in 2015 for lowering greenhouse gas emissions that apply a broad brush to all cities within each respective country. Cities can take ownership of national greenhouse gas emissions and the initiative by setting themselves more stringent urban targets. The target for your city is clean growth based on lower emissions than the Paris Agreement.

It is not reductionist thinking to select three indicators: our outlook should remain holistic and systemic. Reduction does not negate the complexities, but simplification creates clarity. This focus promotes better decision-making and can often make for longer-lived policies. In practice, when we turn to face the right direction we pull other positive changes along with us.

What emerges from the transformation of places and in people is a new kind of prosperity. One that can be measured in aspirational terms of economic progress and not simply economic expansion; of our capacity to thrive, not simply our ability to consume; of realising human potential, not simply preserving the system. These measures lead us to sustainability. It is a far cry from the blind acceptance of Gross National Product as shorthand for our continued wellbeing.

TIPPING POINT

Our global economy is in a state of inherently unstable equilibrium. It is in equilibrium as the forces at work are constantly trying to keep the elements in balance. Mandated, government-led pushes vie with market-driven, company-led pulls. Rich states and powerful multinational organisations strive to protect their stakes in the status quo. The balancing act is dynamic but fundamentally unstable: the current model of economic growth is unjust as too many are excluded, and unsustainable as we have overshot nature's carrying capacity.

According to strategist Roger Martin and Skoll Foundation President, Sally Osberg, national governments have a long track record of driving equilibrium shifts through policy innovation, and companies have a shorter but also impactful track record through their innovation cycles that are driven by profit and the opportunity to provide something new. Strikingly, cities are in a position to change the balance of equilibrium in a way that is neither entirely mandated nor entirely market driven. They are not constrained by the need for ubiquity across an entire country or by the profit imperative. As such, cities can play a unique role in addressing the existing imbalances, and in changing the current conditions under which their citizens live and work. In our urbanised and highly networked world, these localised changes at city level can make a disproportionate difference to our collective fate.

Which way will the equilibrium tip? There is just cause for pessimism. Collectively we are still pursuing the goal of endless economic growth, fully aware that no growth can continue forever and that negative feedback loops in nature inevitably correct the anomaly even if we do not. Runaway climate change is either too terrible to contemplate or the thought paralyses potential action. We are oblivious to the annihilation of other species. For many people, life is already tough and getting tougher. The current narrative is swamped by national politicians and dealmakers whose personal ambitions trump everything else. We end up as the weak link in making change happen, waiting for a new technology to be invented or for a new law to be passed or for a new leader to find a better solution. Powerless, we hold our head in an Edvard Munch scream of angst at a world on the brink of chaos. We do not have the imagination or courage to believe in the new narrative of Darwinian cooperation instead of competition, and do not believe that we have enough power to act. Those that see the present as precarious are considered on the fringe instead of in the vanguard. In the end, we become complicit.

Alternatively we are on the cusp of making up our own minds about transforming the places where we live. The good news is that the problems of partisanship in national politics and the limited, short-term perspectives of shareholders have awakened in us a belief that leadership also matters on a more local level and that we can still make a difference. Humans did not evolve to think naturally on very large scales, which is how we have reached this unstable point globally; to think about issues of such enormity is really no more than a form of abstraction. We live instead by the people and places around us, by the things we can control or experience personally. In the words of the late poet and novelist Charles Bukowski, "You begin saving the world by saving one person at a time; all else is grandiose romanticism or politics."

Civic revolution can finally break the mould. By empowering our cities we can achieve clean growth. By being resourceful we can decouple growth from material consumption. By migrating into cities but staying connected with nature we can regenerate both the urban and wider environment. By inclusion and daring we can rebuild social capital, making cities richer places for all. In regaining our civic sense, each of us attends to the smallness of our city instead of grappling with problems that are beyond the human scale.

As modern societies steer away from government and towards governance, and from hierarchical control to cooperative networks, power is shifting from being concentrated in the past to becoming diffuse in the future. Momentum is building and overcoming the forces of incumbency as cities amplify the efforts of individuals who have the courage to step forward. One new way of doing things opens up possibilities for others to follow in a cascade of consequences. We become the strong link in making change happen in our city, because no one else knows the place where we live and work as well as us. Instead of waiting, we lead this transformation by becoming active citizens and embracing a broader view of prosperity. As a result, the places where we live become the "cities of tomorrow" as we convert them with renewable energy and active transport, enrich them with social spaces and vertical forests, and support them by commoning and with circular economies.

The locus of power marks a very different approach in how we will reach a new equilibrium. Widespread implementation involves a great many localised plans, and in our networked world this speeds up the transition rather than slows it down. As with nature, there is immense power in the proliferation of different designs. When they succeed they are quickly copied. When they fail there are already others in place elsewhere and the downside is limited.

Individuals and communities, in different cities in every country, are implementing a multitude of plans. They are changing the world around us, around the clock. Here are just a few examples of citizens who have chosen to lead and are inspiring a civic revolution that does not sleep:

In Honolulu, USA – Honolulans are implementing a massive Hawaii Fresh Water Initiative that improves the islands' natural ability to capture and store fresh water. It is an encompassing programme that embraces decentralised systems for water capture, encourages significant water reuse and reduces the need for water transmission. As an island people, residents inherently understand the need for a more secure and sustainable water future, and the importance of a wellspring of collaboration to make it happen.

The story of the restoration of Kanewai Spring, one of the last remaining freshwater springs on the island of Oahu, brings the islanders' fresh water initiative to life. The stretch of coastline along Maunalua Bay was once dotted with abundant freshwater springs, each tended by a particular family and passed down through the generations. As the city of Honolulu expanded, these connections were severed and most springs were cut off from the sea. Rediscovering Kanewai Spring, a community group painstakingly restored the spring with the help of elders, fishermen and biologists. According to local resident Max Mukai, "Someday, the fishpond might feed us again. Until that day comes, we're learning so much and gaining as a community from it. Those are our most immediate returns for the restoration work."

In Vancouver, Canada – Vancouverites are competing to make their city the "greenest city in the world" by 2020, focusing on zero carbon, zero waste and healthy ecosystems. The 170 civic programmes span job creation, carbon reduction, natural and built environments, and food. The good news is that it is a race to the top, as other cities also want the honorary title.

Green Bloc Neighbourhoods is one of the community-led programmes that fill the gap between individual-led and city-led change, addressing climate change and resource consumption at city block level. Participants are supported with ideas and implementation, from repair workshops to community swaps to bulk buying to reduce packaging. Neighbourhoods end up decreasing their ecological footprint, and neighbours end up building a stronger sense of community. As one resident commented, "Green Bloc provided an incredible opportunity to build new connections with like-minded people. It encouraged me to take the time to think about what I want for my community's future and act upon it."

In Medellin, Colombia – investing in people, the city is building resilience through social inclusion. Low-income neighbourhoods are an important part of the city's make-up and residents have become more connected by building innovative urban infrastructure, public facilities and community spaces in these areas. Other Latin American cities look at the success of this city's dramatic urban renewal programme to integrate their informal settlements and improve liveability.

The story of Medellin's transformation can be told through many lenses. Comuna 13 is one of sixteen wards in Medellin: it used to be the most popular route through the city for arms and drugs. Today, most of the conflict and violence has been replaced by social investment, job creation and trust. Building a *parque biblioteca*, or library park, in the ward was one of the ideas implemented to create public affluence, helping to rebuild communities and aspirations around recreation, music, art and books. In total, ten *parques biblioteca* were sited in poorer neighbourhoods across the city, drawing in local residents for events and entertainment. Everything they provide is entirely free, sponsored by the city. In the words of one young Colombian from Comuna 13, "I want your final emotion to be that there was a change, and that change is possible."

In Belo Horizonte, Brazil – the city government is providing access to food for every resident, with a municipal food security programme committed to food sovereignty and the right of residents to define their own food and agricultural policies. Belo is recognised as "the city that ended hunger" and a model city for going local to secure a healthy food supply for the future.

There is no set menu to feed growing city populations. In the case of Belo, the system of interconnected programmes is driven by a strong belief that "food is a right" for all city residents. Staple food items are subsidised; food is supplied by the city directly to schools, health clinics and nursing homes; residents are served in city-run *Restaurantes Populares* ("People's Restaurants") where anyone can eat; food vans cater for poor neighbourhoods; farmers' markets are supported throughout the city; food banks distribute excess fresh fruit and vegetables. People look after community gardens and tend fruit trees planted in public spaces; schools grow their own food; families oversee three large commercial gardens in the city that grow organic produce. The high level of public participation in the city programme shows that food is not just about production or municipal policies – it is also an emotive connection to food security and personal health.

In Abidjan, Ivory Coast – Abidjanais are leapfrogging the national electricity grid by choosing off-grid companies that bring them affordable electricity with mini-grids and pay-as-you-go solar home systems. Off-grid power start-ups are pouring into Abidjan and similar cities across the continent to provide tens of millions of city residents with renewable solar energy who have no access to a power grid.

The mindset is liberating: renewable energy is becoming a conventional supply and is no longer considered an alternative technology. Although some of these city dwellers were not using electricity previously, their solar panels decrease pressure on utility companies to build more fossil fuel power plants while replacing polluting kerosene lamps and wood fires. Africa already has more off-grid solar homes than the USA – a promising outlook for a region with huge solar potential and at the forefront of rapid urbanisation. One resident in Abidjan with solar panels smiled as he described the power of word of mouth: "[My neighbour] asked me how it worked. Then he went and bought one of his own."

In Reykjavik, Iceland – sourcing all of their residents' electricity needs from hydropower and geothermal, the city is now working to make all cars and public transit fossil-free by 2040. Elsewhere more than one hundred cities around the world are now mostly powered by renewable energy, demonstrating the power of residents in switching from fossil fuels.

It is possible to turn the world upside down. Less than fifty years ago, Iceland was largely reliant on imported peat and coal to power its homes and businesses. Today, transport is the only power sector that does not rely exclusively on renewables. It is still not enough: switching from petrol and diesel transportation is crucial if Icelanders wish to meet the goals of the Paris Agreement. Clearly they do, as the switch from combustion engine vehicles is now in full swing and charging stations are scrambling to keep up with the demand. According to one expert in Reykjavik, "I think that very soon people will feel it's retrograde to operate a car which you can't plug in, and when we reach that point there is no turning back."

In Pune, India – city residents are transforming their streets into vibrant public spaces with the support of an audacious "complete streets" city programme that embraces continuous footpaths, safe pedestrian crossings, separate cycle tracks, convenient bus stops, organised street vending and appropriately scaled roads. Existing trees are incorporated, benches and art installations added, children's play areas included. Leading the way with its network of complete streets, Pune is one of a hundred cities participating in India's *Smart Cities Mission* urban renewal programme to become more citizen-friendly and sustainable.

Once known as a bicycle city, Pune's bicycles were pushed aside by motorised vehicles until recently. City residents responded so enthusiastically to a new public bike-sharing scheme that the city now has plans to develop seven hundred kilometres of cycle tracks over the next couple of years – encouraging more cycling while reducing traffic congestion and air pollution. To fast track the roll-out, Pune has a partnership approach, with private bicycle-sharing operators supplying the bikes while the city builds the infrastructure and parking. "People have responded positively," commented one Punekar. "Those who were fearing that the city is not ready for such an experiment have been proved wrong."

In Tianjin, China – central government is chasing the ideal of sustainable development as newly constructed eco-cities spring up like mushrooms, with stringent green architectural standards and progressive urban planning and transportation infrastructure. Almost three hundred purpose-built eco-cities are being developed across China to meet the aspirations and reduce the ecological impact of over one hundred million future residents who will migrate from the countryside in the next six years.

Tianjin has started to fill up with residents, as the urban population begins to catch up with an eco-city that has already been built. Any plan for a successful eco-city is ambitious, as it requires changes in people's behaviour that cannot be achieved purely by design. This eco-city may be more fledgling than flagship currently, but it remains a showcase of sustainable ideas within a very ambitious building movement. Such visionary places may still prove to be the best solution for China's rapid urban development. In the words of an investor in yet another new eco-city, "It's like you're watching history happen."

In Christchurch, New Zealand – the city council is pursuing sustainability principles across all areas of governance, similar to other cities across the nation. Connections with nature, circular economies, energy efficiency and energy independence are areas of intense interest for local government and citizen volunteer groups. One of the city's more far-reaching policies is to mitigate the negative impacts on ecosystems, by ensuring all releases into the air, water and soil are non-toxic; food and fibre are harvested from sustainably managed populations; and indigenous biodiversity thrives.

The "Styx Vision" is an exemplar of commoning beyond the city boundary, with people protecting the river Styx catchment area on the northern edge of Christchurch from urban encroachment and harm. The vision of Cantabrians is based on long-term maintenance of the entire spring-fed ecosystem and includes a continuous source-to-sea walkway along the river and a living laboratory focused on learning and research. Ongoing conservation efforts are sustained by like-minded organisations and individuals, whose mantra is to "let these projects mark our human heritage".

From Honolulu to Christchurch, citizens have banded together in the places where they live, reinventing new ways to prosper. Our future will not be conceived or implemented as a unitary inter-national plan; it will be invented in this style: piecemeal, haphazardly, locally. People across hundreds of cities have started this change, and countless more sense the need to take personal action. The future is already here – it is just not very evenly distributed. The tipping point is not simply one of scale: what is missing is not change that is global, but global change that is civic instead of consumerist, collaborative instead of competitive, networked instead of hegemonic.

Cities pull us out of private spaces and into public areas. You cannot help but interact with others at eye level, at street level, at neighbourhood level. The new narrative flourishes because it reinforces the imperatives we must address: you see others who also see the need for change, and they see you. The next stage begins here and now with you, in what you think and how you find new meaning and purpose in your actions. Do not throw away your shot. The only place where you are truly needed is in the city you call home. This has always been the starting point and nowhere else.

Rise up – the tipping point of the civic revolution could be here where you live.

Endnotes

Not every fact in the book has a reference, or else these endnotes would be longer than the main text. Facts that are sourced include quotes, controversial data and statistics. I have organised these sources by chapter rather than by tagging words; the sources offer broad insights to be digested in full and not simply data points to be picked *à la carte*. Sources are provided only when first referenced in the text, and not on any repeated references or for facts that are undisputed and can easily be verified with a keyword search.

SELECT REFERENCES:

TELLING STORIES

Bunzl, M. (2009). 'Geoengineering Research Reservations'. Presentation to the American Association for the Advancement of Science (AAAS), San Diego, 20 February.

Carbon Tracker (2014). 'Unburnable Carbon – Are the World's Financial Markets Carrying a Carbon Bubble?', September.

Cook, J. et al. (2016). 'Consensus on Consensus: a Synthesis of Consensus Estimates on Human-Caused Global Warming'. *Environmental Research Letters*, 11(4), 048002, April.

Cook, J. et al. (2013). 'Quantifying the Consensus on Anthropogenic Global Warming in the Scientific Literature'. *Environmental Research Letters*, doi:10.1088/1748-9326/8/2/024024, January.

Davis, M. (2010). 'Who Will Build the Ark?' *New Left Review* 61, January–February.

Global Carbon Project (2018). 'Carbon Budget and Trends 2017', 12 March. Available online at: www.globalcarbonproject.org/carbonbudget

Gore, A. (2017). *An Inconvenient Sequel – Truth To Power*.

Hansen, J. (2012). 'Why I Must Speak Out About Climate Change'. TED Talk.

Harari, Y. N. (2014). *Sapiens: A Brief History of Humankind*. Harvill Secker, London.

Hawking, S. (2017). 'Stephen Hawking: Expedition New Earth'. Broadcast on BBC 2, U.K., September.

Klein, N. (2014). *This Changes Everything: Capitalism vs. the Climate*. Simon & Schuster, USA.

Meadows, D. H., Meadows, D. L., Randers, J., Behrens III, W. (1972). *The Limits To Growth*. Potomac Associates – Universe Books.

Pauly, D. (1995). 'Anecdotes and the Shifting Baseline Syndrome of Fisheries'. *Trends in Ecology & Evolution*, October.

Rockström, J. et al. (2009). 'Planetary Boundaries: Exploring the Safe Operating Space for Humanity'. *Ecology and Society*, vol. 14, no. 2. JSTOR. Available online at: www.jstor.org/stable/26268316

Seligman, M. E. P. and Tierney, J. (2017). 'We Aren't Built to Live in the Moment'. *New York Times*, Opinion, 19 May.

Semiconductor Industry Association (2015). 'International Technology Roadmap for Semiconductors (ITRS)', 5 June.

Sheeran, P. (2006). 'Does changing cognitions cause health behaviour change?' 20th Conference of the European Health Psychology Society, Warsaw, Poland.

Smith, A. (1776). *The Wealth Of Nations*. W. Strahan and T. Cadell, London.

Teller, A. (2017). 'How to Build Your Own Moonshot Lab'. Interview with Brian Fung, *Washington Post,* 19 April.

The Royal Society (2009). 'Geoengineering the Climate – Science, Governance and Uncertainty', September.

Turner, G. and Alexander, C. (2014). 'Limits to Growth Was Right. New Research Shows We're Nearing Collapse'. The *Guardian,* 2 September.

United Nations (2017). 'World Population Prospects'.

RISING UP

Arendt, H. (1958). *The Human Condition*, 2nd ed. Chicago: University of Chicago Press.

Curtis, P. (2011). 'Reality Check: How Much Did the Banking Crisis Cost Taxpayers?'. The *Guardian* News Blog, 12 September.

Khanna, P. (2016). 'How Megacities are Changing the Map of the World'. TED Talk.

Machiavelli, N. (1520). *Discourse on Reforming the Government of Florence* (Italian: Discorso sopra il riformare lo stato di Firenze).

Olivet, C., Moore, K., Cossar-Gilbert, S., Cingotti, N. (2016). 'The Hidden Costs of RCEP and Corporate Trade Deals in Asia', December.

Schuman, M. (2008). 'Why Detroit is Not Too Big to Fail'. *Time,* 19 December.

Schuman, R. (1950). 'The Schuman Declaration', 9 May.

UN-HABITAT (2016). 'World Cities Report 2016: Urbanization and Development – Emerging Futures'. New York: United Nations. Available online at: https://doi.org/10.18356/d201a997-en

Wimmer, A. and Feinstein, Y. (2010). 'The Rise of the Nation-State Across the World, 1816 to 2001'. *American Sociological Review,* 75(5), pp. 764–90. University of California.

World Bank Group (2010). 'Cities and Climate Change: an Urgent Agenda; Part III – Cities' Contribution To Climate Change', vol. 10, December.

CHANGING DIRECTION

Edenhofer, O., Pichs-Madruga, R., Sokona, Y., Farahani, E., Kadner, S., Seyboth, K., Adler, A., Baum, I., Brunner, S., Eickemeier, P., Kriemann, B., Savolainen, J., Schlömer, S., von Stechow, C., Zwickel, T. and Minx, J. C. (eds.), IPCC (2014). 'Annex IV: Contributors to the IPCC WGIII Fifth Assessment Report'. In: *Climate Change 2014: Mitigation of Climate Change*. Cambridge, U.K. and New York, USA: Cambridge University Press.

Mok, K. (2014). 'Shapeshifted Things: 4D Printed Materials "Programmed" for Self-Transformation'. *The New Stack*, 17 October.

Newman, P. (2017). 'The Internet of Things 2017: Examining How the IoT is Augmenting Workplaces and Lives to Transform the World'. BI Intelligence Report, January.

Randers, J. and Gilding, P. (2010). 'The One Degree War Plan'. *Journal of Global Responsibility*, vol. 1, issue 1, pp.170–188. Available online at: https://doi.org/10.1108/20412561011039762

Schwab, K. (2017). *The Fourth Industrial Revolution*. Crown Publishing Group, New York.

Tibbits, S. (2013). 'The Emergence of "4D Printing"'. TED Talk.

United Nations (2018). 'Revision of World Urbanization Prospects'. Available online at: https://population.un.org/wup

USING POWER

Becker, S. (2013). *Our City, Our Grid: the Energy Remunicipalisation Trend in Germany*, chapter 8. Reclaiming Public Services, EPSU, Amsterdam.

Biello, D. (2008). 'Drilling for Hot Rocks: Google Sinks Cash into Advanced Geothermal Technology'. *Scientific American*, 20 August.

'BP Energy Outlook' (2018). *British Petroleum*. BP Energy Economics.

Burger, C. and Weinmann, J. (2013). *The Decentralized Energy Revolution: Business Strategies for a New Paradigm*. Palgrave Macmillan, U.K.

CDP (formerly the Carbon Disclosure Project). 'The World's Renewable Energy Cities'. Report and data sets available online at: www.cdp.net

Carrington, D. (2017). 'G20 Public Finance for Fossil Fuels "Is Four Times More Than Renewables"'. The *Guardian*, 5 July.

Chow, L. (2017). '1 Million Plastic Bottles Bought Every Minute, That's Nearly 20,000 Every Second'. *EcoWatch*, June.

City of Amsterdam. 'Circular Innovation Programme 2016–18' (in Dutch).

Ellen MacArthur Foundation (2017). 'Cities in the Circular Economy – an Initial Exploration'.

Ellen MacArthur Foundation and McKinsey & Company (2014). 'Towards the Circular Economy: Accelerating the Scale-Up Across Global Supply Chains'. World Economic Forum, January.

Gladek, E., van Odijk, S., Theuws, P., Herder, A. (2015). 'Circular Buiksloterham'. CC-BY-NC-ND 2014 Metabolic, Studioninedots & DELVA Landscape Architects, March.

Jacobson, M. Z. and Delucchi, M. A. et al. (2017). '100% Clean and Renewable Wind, Water, and Sunlight All-Sector Energy Roadmaps for 139 Countries of the World'. *Joule*, vol. 1, issue 1, September. Available online at: http://dx.doi.org/10.1016/j.joule.2017.07.005

Levi, M. (2013). *Climatic Change*, 118: 609. Available online at: https://doi.org/10.1007/s10584-012-0658-3

MacKay, D. J. C. (2008). 'Sustainable Energy – Without the Hot Air'. UIT Cambridge. ISBN 978-0-9544529-3-3. Available online at: www.withouthotair.com

Myers, J. (2016). 'How Do the World's Biggest Companies Compare to the Biggest Economies?'. World Economic Forum, 19 October.

Nathwani, J., Blackstock, J. et al. (2012). 'Equinox Blueprint: Energy 2030'. Waterloo Global Science Initiative, February.

Pickard, S. and Granoff, I. (2015). 'Can Carbon Capture and Storage Justify New Coal-Fired Electricity?' Overseas Development Institute (ODI), December.

Punyte, I. (2017). WASTED – a community initiative to foster collaborative waste separation'. *Cities in Transition*, April. Available online at: www.citiesintransition.eu

Shirai, T. and Adam, Z. (2017). 'Commentary: Fossil Fuel Consumption Subsidies are Down, but Not Out'. International Energy Agency, 20 December.

Sterling, B. (2016). 'Fracking and Methane'. *Wired*, 24 March 2016. Available online at: https://www.wired.com/beyond-the-beyond/2016/03/fracking-and-methane

U.S. Energy Information Administration (2018). 'U.S. Crude Oil and Natural Gas Rotary Rigs in Operation', 28 September.

World Economic Forum (2016). 'The New Plastics Economy – Rethinking the Future of Plastics', January.

SAVING LIFE

Barbu, A-D. (EEA), Griffiths, N. and Morton, G. (Ricardo-AEA) (2013). 'Achieving energy efficiency through behaviour change: what does it take?' European Environment Agency Technical Report No 5.

Bauwens, M. and Onzia, Y. (2017). 'Commons Transition Plan for the City of Ghent'.

BBC News (2018). 'The 11 Cities Most Likely to Run Out of Drinking Water – Like Cape Town', 11 February. Available online at: https://www.bbc.co.uk/news/world-42982959

Beiser, V. (2018). *The World in a Grain: The Story of Sand and How It Transformed Civilization*. Penguin Random House, New York.

Brown, D. (2017). 'Challenging the conceptual boundaries of the compact city paradigm in sub-Saharan Africa: Towards Southern alternatives'. DPU Working Paper 187, ISSN 1474-3280, March. London, U.K.: the Development Planning Unit, The Bartlett, University College London.

City of New York (2016). 'OneNYC: Mayor de Blasio Announces Major New Steps to Dramatically Reduce NYC Buildings' Greenhouse Gas Emissions', 22 April. Available online at: www1.nyc.gov

Crawford, J. (2012). 'What if the World's Soil Runs Out?' *Time*, 14 December.

Erickson, P. and Tempest, K. (2015). 'Keeping Cities Green: Avoiding Carbon Lock-In Due to Urban Development'. Stockholm Environment Institute, Working Paper 2015–11.

Euroalter (2017). Interview with Mayor of the City of Ghent, Daniel Termont. *European Alternatives*, 27 February. Available online at: www.euroalter.com

Forest Research UK (2008). 'Green Infrastructure and the Urban Heat Island'. Evidence note.

Gleeson, T. et al. (2016). 'The Global Volume and Distribution of Modern Groundwater'. *Nature Geoscience*, vol. 9, pp. 161–7.

Jacobs, J. (1961). *The Death and Life of Great American Cities*.

Jakuboski, S. (2015). 'Green Science: Musings of a Young Conservationist', January. Available online at: www.nature.com

Kallakuri, C., Vaidyanathan, S., Kelly, M., Cluett, R. (2016). 'The 2016 International Energy Efficiency Scorecard'. American Council for an Energy-Efficient Economy, Research Report E1602, 19 July.

Kolczak, A. (2017). 'This City Aims to be the World's Greenest'. *National Geographic*, 28 February.

Leenes, G. et al. (2007). 'Water Neutrality: a Concept Paper', November. Available online at: www.researchgate.net

Lovasi, G. S. et al. (2018). 'Children Living in Areas with More Street Trees Have Lower Prevalence of Asthma'. *Journal of Epidemiology and Community Health*, 62.7, pp. 647–9. PMC, 5 October.

Ludacer, R. (2018). 'The World is Running Out of Sand'. *Business Insider UK*, 11 June.

Lunde, M. (2015). *The History of Bees*. Scribner, U.K.

McDonald, R. et al. (2017). 'Funding Trees for Health: an Analysis of Finance and Policy Actions to Enable Tree Planting for Public Health'. The Nature Conservancy.

Millennium Ecosystem Assessment (2003). 'Ecosystems and Human Well-being: a Framework for Assessment'. Island Press. Available at: www.millenniumassessment.org

Nowak, D. (2002). *The Effects of Urban Trees on Air Quality*. Syracuse, NY, USA: USDA Forest Service.

Ostrom, E. (2015). *Governing the Commons – the Evolution of Institutions for Collective Action*. Cambridge, UK: Cambridge University Press.

Padowski, J. C. and Gorelick, S. M. (2014). 'Global Analysis of Urban Surface Water Supply Vulnerability'. *Environmental Research Letters*, 9 104004.

Peters, A. (2016). 'Madrid is Covering Itself in Plants to Help Fight Rising Temperatures'. *FastCompany*, 3 February.

Secretariat of the Convention on Biological Diversity (2012). 'Cities and Biodiversity Outlook'. Montreal, 64 pages. Available online at: www.cbd.int

Shove, E. and Spurling, N. (eds.) (2013). *Sustainable Practices: Social Theory and Climate Change*. London, UK: Routledge.

Wilson, M. (2016). 'The City of Tomorrow is a Petri Dish – By Design'. *FastCompany*, 11 March. Available online at: www.fastcompany.com

Wohlleben, P. (2015). *The Hidden Life of Trees: What they Feel, How they Communicate*. Greystone Books, Canada.

DISCOVERING RICHNESS

Abers, R., Brandão, I., King, R. and Votto, D. (2018). 'Porto Alegre: Participatory Budgeting and the Challenge of Sustaining Transformative Change'. World Resources Report Case Study. Washington, DC, USA: World Resources Institute. Available online at: www.citiesforall.org

Bond, B. and Exley, Z. (2016). *Rules for Revolutionaries: How Big Organizing Can Change Everything*. Chelsea Green Publishing, USA.

Burden, A. (2014). 'How Public Spaces Make Cities Work'. TED Talk.

Centre for Public Impact (2016). 'The Metrocable: Transport by Urban Cable Car in Medellín'. Case study, 25 March. Available online at: www.centreforpublicimpact.org

Cooke, J. (2018). 'The Impossible Possible City – How Mexico City's Urban Innovation Lab Tackles the City's Challenges'. *Curbed*, 18 April. Available online at: www.curbed.com

Duany Plater-Zyberk & Company (1999). *The Lexicon of the New Urbanism*. Miami, USA: Duany Plater-Zyberk & Company.

Ellen MacArthur Foundation (2015). 'Growth Within: a Circular Economy Vision for a Competitive Europe'.

Glaeser, E. L. and Kahn, M. E. (2004). 'Sprawl and Urban Growth'. *Handbook of Regional and Urban Economics*, edn. 1, vol. 4.

Holt-Lunstad, J., Smith, T. B., Layton, J. B. (2010). 'Social Relationships and Mortality Risk: a Meta-analytic Review'. *PLoS Medicine*, 7(7): e1000316. Available online at: https://doi.org/10.1371/journal.pmed.1000316

Jakhar, P. (2018). 'Who Really Came Up With China's "Four New Inventions"?', BBC Monitoring, April.

Kelbie, P. (2003). 'Rise in Gated Communities Could Pose a Threat to Public Services'. The *Independent*, 27 September.

Lefevre, B. and Enriquez, A. (2014). 'Transport Sector Key to Closing the World's Emissions Gap'. World Resources Institute, 19 September. Available online at: www.wri.org

Malhotra, A. (2017). 'Can the Affluent Be Convinced to Ride Transit in Delhi?'. *CityLab*, 11 December.

Mayor of London (2018). 'The London Plan – the Spatial Development Strategy for London'. Available online at: www.london.gov.uk

Rukmini, S. (2015). 'India Walks To Work: Census'. *The Hindu*, New Delhi, 14 November.

The Economist (2018). 'Self-Driving Cars Will Require New Business Models'. *The Economist* Special Report, 1 March. Available online at: www.economist.com

Transport for London (TfL) and Mayor of London (2017). 'Analysis of Cycling Potential 2016'. Policy Analysis Report, March.

United Nations (2018). 'World Urbanization Prospects 2018'. Available online at: https://population.un.org/wup

INSPIRING REVOLUTION

Bavier, J. (2018). 'Off-grid Solar Energy Takes Root in West Africa'. Reuters, 20 February.

CDP (2018). 'Over 100 Global Cities Get Majority of Electricity from Renewables', 27 February. Available online at: www.cdp.net

Chan, L., Hillel, O., Elmqvist, T., Werner, P., Holman, N., Mader, A. and Calcaterra, E. (2014). *User's Manual on the Singapore Index on Cities' Biodiversity* (also known as the City Biodiversity Index). Singapore: National Parks Board, Singapore. Available online at: www.cbd.int

Chappell, M. J. (2018). *Beginning to End Hunger – Food and the Environment in Belo Horizonte, Brazil, and Beyond*. University of California Press.

City of Vancouver. 'Greenest City: 2020 Action Plan'. Available online at: www.vancouver.ca

Evergreen British Columbia. 'Green Bloc Neighbourhoods'. Available online at: www.evergreen.ca

Fossaert, P. and Morales, J. (2014). 'Medellín's Metamorphosis – an Interview with Mayor Aníbal Gaviría'. McKinsey Center for Government, May.

Global Footprint Network. 'Ecological Footprint'. Available online at www.footprintnetwork.org

Government of Kiribati. 'National Biodiversity Strategies and Action Plan 2016–20'. Available online at: www.cbd.int

Greenhouse Gas Protocol. 'Global Protocol for Community-Scale Greenhouse Gas Emission Inventories – An Accounting and Reporting Standard for Cities'. Available online at: www.ghgprotocol.org

Hawai'i Community Foundation (2015). 'A Blueprint for Action – Water Security for an Uncertain Future (2016–18)'. Available online at: www.hawaiicommunityfoundation.org

Hrafnsdóttir, H. (2016). 'Reykjavík Carbon Neutral by 2040'. Department of Environment and Planning, Reykjavik City, 13 October. Available online at: www.intelligenttransport.com

Iceland Magazine (2017). 'Fourth of All New Cars in Iceland Now Electric Vehicles'. *Iceland Magazine*, 22 November.

Ismail, N. (2018). 'Smart Cities in India: Embracing the Opportunity of Urbanisation'. *Information Age, Smart Cities*, 7 August. Available online at: www.information-age.com

Kennedy, R. F. (1968). Robert F. Kennedy Speeches, Remarks at the University of Kansas, 18 March. Available online at: www.jfklibrary.org

Lewis, C. (2017). 'Happiness Before Profit: Bhutan Seeks to Redefine Business Using Buddhist Values'. *Buddhistdoor Global*, 15 December. Available online at: www.buddhistdoor.net

Martin, R. and Osberg. S. (2015). *Getting Beyond Better: How Social*

Entrepreneurship Works. Harvard Business Review Press, Boston Massachusetts.

Naushad, N. (2017). 'Vibrant Pune: City's Streets Transform into Vital Public Spaces'. Institute for Transportation & Development Policy. Available online at: www.itdp.in

Quinn, P. (2013). 'After Devastating Tornado, Town is Reborn "Green"'. *USA TODAY, Green Living* magazine, 25 April .

Rocha, C. and Lessa, I. (2010). 'Urban Governance for Food Security: the Alternative Food System in Belo Horizonte, Brazil'. *International Planning Studies*, 14:4, pp. 389–400.

Schmidt, L. (2018). 'Unsettled Partners: How Colombia's Most Notorious Neighborhood Has Now Become Its Pride'. Unsettled.

Shanmugaratnam, T. (2017). 'Tianjin Eco-City a Role Model'. *The Straits Times*, 26 June.

Shepard, W. (2008). 'China's 5 Most Amazing 'New' Cities'. *Wanderlust*, 17 April 2008. Available online at: www.wanderlust.co.uk

The Trust for Public Land (2018). 'For Honolulu Residents, Reviving a Forgotten Spring is a Labor of Love', 1 February. Available online at: www.tpl.org

United Nations Climate Change. The Paris Agreement. Available online at: www.unfccc.int

Wellington City Council. 'Wellington 2040'. Available online at: www. wgtn2040.govt.nz

World Health Organization (2018). WHO Global Ambient Air Quality Database (update). Available online at: www.who.int/airpollution

Acknowledgements

This book is by no means a complete picture, only a direction. I have tried to corral numerous insights, together with my own informed thinking, in order to stir up people's imagination and advance some of the current arguments. The result has been the rediscovery of the incredible potential of our civic power at a pivotal moment. It is also a realisation that this is a journey not a destination, and will always be a work in progress.

From concept to completion, this book has been over a year in the making. I wish to express my gratitude to Lord Davies and the other panel judges, who shortlisted my hastily submitted essay for the inaugural Indigo Prize in economics. They gave me the encouragement to grow the seed of an idea about a better way to measure the wealth of modern nations into a more grounded, civic perspective on prosperity and what we need to do differently.

I am immensely grateful to Sir Tim Smit, who brought both his humanity and his intellect to the foreword. As the co-founder of the Eden Project, he is a truly inspirational figure. The Eden Project is a powerful symbol of ordinary people working together to achieve the near-impossible. It is the epitome of the spirit of this citizen's guide and the hope that we too can achieve amazing things.

I attended the London School of Economics and Political Science during the summer of 2018, while researching and writing this book. I am indebted to my learned professors – Savvas Verdis, Ricky Burdett, Philipp Rode and Tony Travers – who shared their wisdom on London and global cities, and challenged my thinking on city governance, planning and design.

The manuscript was read in its entirety several times by Helen Owers, and her comments led to significant improvements in both its substance and organisation. I would like to thank her for her generous contribution. Many other people shared their valuable comments with me on different parts of this book. I would like to thank in particular Andy Knott, Shashank Mani Tripathi and Sharon Stulberg.

It is one thing to put pen to paper, quite another to publish a book. I am fortunate to have worked with the publishing team at Matador who cheerfully and professionally guided the manuscript through the process. They have made this publication much better than it would have been otherwise, and the remaining deficiencies are my responsibility.

Lastly, a personal thank you to my dearest. To Heather, who was my first editor, is my better half, and will always be my inspiration. She gave me the time and space to write when there was none to give. To Oliver and Andrea, for every day. Their generation will inherit the world we leave behind.